T0326362

Toni Erdmann

German Film Classics

Series Editors

Gerd Gemünden, Dartmouth College
Johannes von Moltke, University of Michigan

Advising Editors

Anton Kaes, University of California-Berkeley
Eric Rentschler, Harvard University

Editorial Board

Hester Baer, University of Maryland
Mattias Frey, University of Kent
Rembert Hüser, Goethe University, Frankfurt
Claudia Lenssen, Journalist and Film Critic, Berlin
Cristina Nord, Berlinale Forum
Brad Prager, University of Missouri
Reinhild Steingröver, Eastman School of Music

Also in the series:

TONI ERDMANN

GERD GEMÜNDEN

CAMDEN HOUSE

First published 2021 by Camden House

Camden House is an imprint of Boydell & Brewer Inc.
668 Mt. Hope Avenue, Rochester, NY 14620, USA
and of Boydell & Brewer Limited
PO Box 9, Woodbridge, Suffolk IP12 3DF, UK
www.boydellandbrewer.com

Cover image reproduced by kind permission
of Komplizen Film, 2020.

ISBN-13: 978-1-64014-109-4

Library of Congress Cataloging-in-Publication Data

CIP data is available from the Library of Congress.

This publication is printed on acid-free paper.
Printed in the United States of America.

Publication of this book was supported by a grant from the
German Film Institute (GFI) of the University of Michigan
Department of Germanic Languages & Literatures.

CONTENTS

ACKNOWLEDGMENTS

This is a small book, but some big thanks are in order. First and foremost, there are my series co-editor Johannes von Moltke and Camden House editorial director Jim Walker. Both not only encouraged me to switch roles from editor to author, but also provided the same rigorous and constructive criticism with which they guide our other Camden House authors. I am also indebted to the anonymous reader, who made numerous valuable suggestions, and to Bruce Duncan, who worked through the entire manuscript with a very fine comb. Hester Baer's research on neoliberal German cinema provided crucial impulses, as did the pioneering work of many of my colleagues (friends, really) who have written on the Berlin School. A big thank-you must go to Maren Ade and her colleagues at Komplizen Film, who early on trusted me with the screenplay to *Toni Erdmann* and who fielded many questions and queries. Chris Ivanyi, a multi-media lab technician at Dartmouth's Jones Media Center, offered crucial help with illustrations, while showing great patience with my Zoom skills.

While I was fortunate to have concluded my research for this book just prior to when the coronavirus pandemic made access to archives and libraries impossible, the majority of the manuscript was written during lockdown in New Hampshire and Berlin. The daily writing routine came to provide a sense of structure and concentration when both were threatening to slip away. Always my first reader in more ways than one, Silvia Spitta provided the right dose of criticism and encouragement to keep me at my desk, but also to help me navigate these uncertain times and keep life meaningful.

Toni Erdmann

A Question of Performance

About twenty minutes into *Toni Erdmann*, Maren Ade's tragicomedy about the strained relationship between Ines Conradi, a young business consultant working in Bucharest, and her father Winfried, a retired music teacher and compulsive prankster, Winfried meets Ines's personal assistant, Anca. Winfried has just arrived on an unannounced visit in the Romanian capital, catching his overworked daughter in the midst of a busy schedule. Anca is dispatched to meet Winfried and help him settle in while her boss shuffles between meetings. Their brief encounter provides a lovely sketch of the sort of strains that linguistic, cultural, and generational differences put on mutual understanding. Switching between German and English, since both conversation partners seem skeptical about the other's foreign language skills, Anca rattles off a list of five-star hotels and their amenities for Winfried to choose from. Clearly planning to stay at his daughter's place, he tells her, "I'm only the father." Clueless about what his daughter's career is actually about, Winfried is eager to know how Ines behaves as a boss. "Ms. Conradi is very honest," Anca explains, and "she gives me a lot of feedback about my performance." "Performance," Winfried wonders, "this describes your job?" "No," Anca replies, adding that the term actually describes her duties "in general, in meetings, with the team, dealing with clients." It is obvious that for Winfried, who comes from the world of music and the stage, the term *performance* has a circumscribed meaning that has little to do with the kind of professional strictures Anca describes.

Toni Erdmann is peppered with a variety of bizarre and outrageous performances, and it is in this brief exchange that the term's diverging meanings are first established. For Anca, and especially

"Performance . . . this describes your job?"

for Ines, an effective performance is crucial for meeting the unyielding expectations of the neoliberal economy. To the two women, performance, which includes command over facial expressions, gestures, and body language, stands for everything that, when combined with the proper attire, creates an appearance that hides thoughts and feelings. Being able to look blank, bland, and inscrutable—presenting the proverbial poker face—is a must for productive business negotiations. This concept of performance not only enables professional success; it becomes synonymous with it.[1]

For Winfried, by contrast, performance is what makes it possible to become someone other than ourselves. By putting on a mask, we alter our identity or pretend to be someone else altogether. Thus, while the business world's performance is singular, with clearly measurable results, Winfried thinks of performances as being manifold activities that open up a space for the imagination rather than closing it down, and that invite us to wonder, "what if"? Rather than being an act of grueling self-discipline and self-effacement, in Winfried's hands performance becomes anarchic role-play that is meant to disrupt the standardization of (his daughter's) life.

Soul mates: Winfried's makeup matches his dog Willi.

By the time we witness his conversation with Anca, we have already seen a few examples of Winfried's performances. In an early scene, he directs a school choir composed of children with faces painted like the grim reaper singing a merry song about death for a retiring teacher. While still wearing the same makeup, he visits his aging mother who barely raises an eyebrow at this apparition, and he then attends his ex-wife Renate's welcome party for Ines, where he promptly smears some of his makeup on her business blazer—a small imprint that anticipates the big impact his visit to Bucharest will have. It is during this first encounter between father and daughter that the two notions of performance first collide. Ines's icy reaction, which barely acknowledges Winfried's faux pas, is an example of the extraordinary self-control she has internalized. The first shot of her, taken through a window of her mother's house as she is making a business call on the veranda, had already cast her as spatially and psychologically removed. She remains reserved during brief, polite chitchat with Winfried and Renate, and apologizes for not having time to visit her grandmother, Winfried's elderly mother. Only in Bucharest will the viewer come to understand that what

Ines is spatially and emotionally removed from her family.

appears to be a personal trait is in fact a coping mechanism for her career's exacting demands.

In contrast to Ines's apparent unapproachability and aloofness, Winfried is an extrovert whose penchant for role-play has already been established in the very first scene of the film, in which a courier tries to deliver a package. The unsuspecting man quickly becomes the butt of Winfried's over-the-top impersonation of his "brother Toni," who has allegedly been recently released from prison where he had served time for making mail bombs. Dressed up in a bathrobe with sunglasses, bare-chested, and with a banana in hand, from which a handcuff dangles, Winfried/Toni accepts the package by dryly stating, "thanks so much, I'm really looking forward to defusing this." The impact of the scene plays out in the countenance of the overtasked mail carrier, who struggles to keep a straight face, especially when Winfried's heart rate monitor suddenly emits a beeping sound. Employing a handheld camera and lasting more than three minutes, this opening takes a prolonged view at the surreal and absurd nature of the everyday. The outrageous scene is cast in

Toni makes his first entrance.

a cool and detached visual style that suggests banality, a contrast in tone that *Toni Erdmann*, in ever-amplified fashion, will explore and exploit for the entirety of its 162-minute running time.

On a general level, then, performance serves as the film's central metaphor for the diverging identities and self-understandings of Ines and Winfried, and for how the two different generations define the meaning of life, happiness, and death. In a more concrete sense, performance becomes a rivaling practice through which father and daughter stage their conflict, alternating between competing with, and becoming complicit in, ever more daring and outrageous scenarios. The result is a story that is by turns hilarious, cringeworthy, and heart-wrenching and that encompasses comedy and tragedy in equal measure. Propelled by nuanced performances from Sandra Hüller (as Ines) and Peter Simonischek (as her father), *Toni Erdmann* traverses a remarkable range of moods and emotions. Indeed, without this third meaning of performance—the extraordinary acting of the main cast, which will be explored in detail—the film would not work. Ultimately, the film's generational tug-of-war provides profound insights into the precarity of life; into the redefinition of feminism by the children of the generation of 1968; and into reconfigured East-West relations in post-Wall Europe. Lastly, in light of Ade's artisanal mode of filmmaking, in which she regularly assumes the role of writer, director, and producer, *Toni Erdmann* becomes a highly self-reflexive comment on the neoliberal dictates of global art cinema.

A Cannes Sensation

The film opens on Winfried and his monotonous life as a retired teacher in Aachen. A certain emptiness marks his everyday: Winfried is divorced (while his ex-wife seems happily remarried), his last remaining piano student quits his lessons, and his elderly mother Annegret seems fine without his care. Time seems to have stood still for Winfried, a mildly eccentric loner whose jokes amuse no one. The death of his ailing dog prompts him to make an unannounced visit to Bucharest. Winfried's unstated mission is to reconnect with a daughter who has somehow slipped away from him. When he realizes that Ines finds very little time for him, the prankster in him begins to disrupt her professional activities. After a standoff about the meaning of life, which occurs about an hour into the film, Winfried departs as suddenly as he had appeared. With the father gone, the focus of the film shifts to Ines, whom we observe in high-powered business negotiations on behalf of her client, Henneberg, who is planning a takeover of a failing oil production company. During a girls' night out, Ines and her friends Tatjana and Steph kvetch about who has had the worst weekend, with Ines claiming the prize owing to her having to deal with her impossible father. It is at this point that a certain Toni Erdmann (Winfried in a shaggy black wig and wearing protruding fake teeth) interrupts the conversation on which he has secretly been eavesdropping. Ines plays along, perhaps because she is too shocked or embarrassed to give Winfried away, or because she feels challenged to outperform her father. What ensues is an ever-more daring game of chicken in which father and daughter steadily up the ante to get under each other's skin. Building toward a dramatic climax, the film's third act consists of four set pieces that take their relationship, and the film, to new levels. These involve a karaoke performance, extended nudity, a hairy embrace, and a heart-wrenching coda, when Ines returns to Germany to attend her grandmother's funeral and the reunion with her father becomes the occasion for one last emotional performance.

When the film premiered at the 2016 Cannes Film Festival, it became an unexpected overnight sensation. During the first press screening, there was frenetic applause mid-scene during Hüller's karaoke performance, something virtually unheard of among seasoned critics.[2] The next day, the *Hollywood Reporter* effused, "Here is the world's first genuinely funny, 162-minute German comedy of embarrassment," while Guy Lodge, in *Variety*, spoke of a "humane, hilarious triumph."[3] "Long after this year's juries have disbanded and the world has forgotten who won this year's award," Manohla Dargis added in the *New York Times*, "the 2016 edition will best be remembered as the year Ms. Ade gave us *Toni Erdmann*, a work of great beauty, great feeling, and great cinema."[4]

The film's nomination had already been considered a major breakthrough and had garnered considerable media attention in Germany. The last German entry to compete at Cannes had been Wim Wenders's *Palermo Shooting* in 2008, and if one considers the historically notorious underrepresentation of women at the festival, the selection of Ade's film was a near miracle. When the festival jury overlooked *Toni Erdmann* for the Palme d'Or, the decision clearly differed from that of critics and general audiences, and most observers felt that sexism had won again, noting that the only woman to take a top prize at Cannes remains Jane Campion for *The Piano* in 1993.

The enthusiasm created at Cannes has only grown in the years since. *Toni Erdmann* became a resounding critical success, first in Germany and then internationally. The film grossed more than five million euros domestically (then $5.5 million), and it was sold into more than one hundred countries, including the most important European markets, the United States, Russia, Hong Kong, and several Latin American countries. Among its many recognitions— as of current count, seventy-nine nominations and fifty-five wins— are the Cannes FIPRESCI Award, the European Film Award, the German Film Prize, as well as an Academy Award nomination for best foreign picture. Soon after the Oscars, Ade's production company, Komplizen Film, sold the rights for a Hollywood remake. Now more than five years old, the film seems to have established itself as an internationally acclaimed classic of recent cinema. In the 2020 *Film Comment* ranking of the previous decade's top fifty films, *Toni Erdmann* claimed second place.[5]

The overwhelming majority of both German and international critics were surprised by the film's sensational success, and even the director and her team were not prepared for what happened during the course of the Cannes festival and afterward. Yet in many ways *Toni Erdmann* builds on Ade's first two features as director and writer, as well as on her work as a producer. Her 2003 breakout feature, *Der Wald vor lauter Bäumen* (*The Forest for the Trees*), won the Sundance Jury Award, making it an impressive debut that prompted critic and filmmaker Kent Jones to note, "if I had to point to one young filmmaker in the world whose future seems to me the brightest, it would be Maren."[6] Already Ade's follow-up, *Alle anderen* (*Everybody Else*) made good on Jones's prediction. It was awarded Silver Bears for the Grand Jury Prize and for Best Actress, for Birgit Minichmayr, at the 2009 Berlinale, and elevated Ade into the small group of internationally recognized contemporary German directors. The film sold two hundred thousand tickets in Germany, an impressive figure by domestic standards, which greatly helped finance *Toni Erdmann*.

Ade's first two features share with *Toni Erdmann* a focus on young female professionals who try to establish their identity vis-à-vis their parents' generation, even if these parents are not really present in the two earlier films. *The Forest for the Trees* revolves around a young schoolteacher, Melanie (Eva Löbau), who moves to a new city to accept her first job. Eager to introduce "a breath of fresh air" into somewhat stale classroom routines, Melanie meets with resistance from her more traditional and significantly older colleagues. Socially awkward and overeager to please those around her, the newcomer soon finds herself completely isolated in a narrow and confined world, not unlike the business elite in Bucharest in whose circles Ines will find herself. Melanie's mother, like Winfried, rightfully suspects that her daughter is lonely "in der Fremde" (far from home), even if the foreign lands referred to here are only a one-hour drive from her hometown. *Everybody Else*, too, takes place far from home—namely, on the bucolic island of Sardinia—where Gitti (Minichmayr) and her boyfriend Chris (Lars Eidinger) hang out at his parents' vacation home. Young urban professionals from Berlin, they spend their vacation wondering who they are or ought to be, and what they are to each other.

If in *Toni Erdmann* Winfried/Toni explicitly puts his daughter into awkward situations that purposely and publicly embarrass her, the notion of feeling ashamed or embarrassed is also central for the two earlier films. *A Forest for the Tress*, in particular, is loaded with cringeworthy moments, as the audience feels constantly embarrassed by, and for, Melanie, who is oblivious to what others think of her. Indeed, the less aware she is of how embarrassing her behavior is, the more intensely viewers feel ashamed on her behalf, generating what Germans call *fremdschämen*. Yet Melanie is also a deeply sincere and well-meaning person whose shortcomings we cannot condemn; instead of feeling superior to her, we share her pain and loneliness. Like Ade's other main characters, Melanie never becomes a caricature but is painted in sympathetic shades of gray.

In *Everybody Else*, too, the notion of embarrassing behavior is central, but it plays out somewhat differently. Hyperaware young urban professionals, Gitti and Chris are at pains to avoid embarrassing moments. To prevent this, they both adopt a tone of pervasive irony that becomes a permanent performance of detachment. As Marco Abel has perceptively stated, this irony is meant "to block moments of embarrassment."[7] As a result, Gitti and Chris are constantly on high alert not to conform to what they perceive as traditional expectations associated with gender, professional success, or a "healthy" relationship. Yet this detachment also leads to making their respective performances illegible to each other. When Chris, for example, puts his arm around Gitti, she begins to laugh. When he asks her why she's laughing, she takes his arm off her shoulder and responds, "Because you're such a terrible actor. . . . With your arm. You've never done this before." As Abel notes, as viewers we have no reason to assume that Chris's gesture was a contrived or exaggerated performance of masculine sheltering, but we have also already learned that Gitti is straightforward and speaks her mind, and we are thus completely unsure whether any form of role-playing was happening here or not. Another telling scene occurs when Chris shows their dinner guests Hans and Sana his parents' home, making a mockery of the kitschy tchotchkes that his mother has collected. Showcasing his mother's "bad taste" allows Chris not to feel embarrassed by her collection and to furthermore assume a position of superiority, but the strategy backfires when Sana completely identifies with the mother's trinkets, which Chris must stop ridiculing because he needs Hans's professional support.

Both *Everybody Else* and *The Forest for the Trees* gain their emotional impact through the extraordinary performance of their lead characters, whose confined setting—be it a provincial German city or a Mediterranean island—puts them at the center of what feels like a chamber play. While Löbau plays off of a number of supporting characters—among them a dull colleague who is attracted to her and a neighbor who befriends her but soon tires of her—*Everybody Else* is essentially a two-hander. Propelled by a marvelous Eidinger and Minichmayr, we follow Chris and Gitti through their daily discussions and squabbles about work, sexuality, and the meaning of life. Like Hüller and Simonischek, these actors first became known for their theater work (even if by now they are, like Hüller, also sought-after film professionals). Even though Ade's films do not resemble plays, her cinema revolves centrally around her work with the actors and the script. As she has explained, up to two years of preparing each feature are taken up by the writing of the script, often with the roles already cast. Before shooting begins, the director then rehearses extensively with the main cast on location. In contrast to full-time film actors, "theater actors," Ade has remarked, "are used to a long rehearsal process and to taking responsibility."[8]

This focus on the actors' subtleties also plays out in the construction of the three films' respective plot lines. In all of them, individual scenes often tend to run for an extended period (a naked brunch scene in *Toni Erdmann* clocks in at over ten minutes). Scenes often begin when a character enters a room, and then the camera follows her and those she interacts with for a prolonged time. This duration is necessary, Ade has explained, for the emergence of what happens between the lines: "The surface is actually trite. What really matters takes place on the level of the subtext. Going into rehearsals, I do not know what will work until I've actually seen it acted out: where does the intensity lie, where is the greatest pain, where are the emotionally strongest contrasts?"[9] In particular, Ade's healthy dose of humor reveals itself only slowly, as the films unfold, and it becomes clear that what at first might appear as superficial is the result of careful attention to detail. In *Toni Erdmann*, the third act harvests what the first act has carefully planted; or, as Sean Burns puts it, it's a film with a "very, very long fuse."[10]

This sense of a false superficiality is further enhanced through a sober visual style that does not draw attention to itself. In general, Ade's films begin in medias res, avoiding traditional establishing shots or quickly introduced backstories that would let audiences situate the characters in a concrete time and place. Eschewing fancy dolly shots, pans, zooms, or slow-motion photography, the camera is less a chronicler than an eavesdropper. As noted, scenes play out at a slow pace and reveal their inner dynamic only over time, while unobtrusive editing, by Ade's longtime collaborator Heike Parplies, does not detract from the precision of the leading cast's acting. All of Ade's films employ a significant amount of handheld camera, yet as Richard Brody has aptly observed, Ade's use of that device is very different from that of other directors. Reviewing *Toni Erdmann*, he notes that here the "handheld camera style is neither as agile and probing as a handheld camera can be nor as analytically poised or incisively composed as a camera fixed in place can be. [Ade] mainly follows actors at a clear and comfortable middle distance."[11] Beyond a lot of handheld camera, *The Forest for the Trees* also features "poor" light, creating an unglamorous look for showcasing a rather bland life. The point bears repetition that beneath banality lie meaning and purpose. As Manohla Dargis has remarked regarding *Everybody Else*, Ade's style is "at once laid-back and rigorous. Ms. Ade doesn't telegraph her intentions, letting gestures, glances, seemingly unrelated events and offhanded remarks gather force."[12]

Ade's visual style and storytelling preferences, together with her professional training at a premier German film school, have led her to be considered a key member of the Berlin School. (A still from *Everybody Else* adorns the 2013 MoMA publication on the Berlin School, signaling Ade's central position in this grouping of key contemporary German directors.) While the historical formation and current development of that important movement will be discussed in more detail below, I want to sketch Ade's training and professional background, as well as her collaborations with fellow students and other key members of the Berlin School. Born in 1976 in the southwestern city of Karlsruhe, Ade was already experimenting as a teenager with a Hi-8 camcorder. In 1998, she enrolled at the Hochschule für Fernsehen und Film (University of Television and

Film; hereafter referred to as HFF) in Munich. One of her teachers at the HFF was Doris Dörrie, one of Germany's most popular and commercially successful directors of comedies and relationship dramas. (It is important to note, though, that Ade's sense of comedy is distinctly different from Dörrie's mainstream sensibility.) Other important fellow Munich students included Sonja Heiss, Benjamin Heisenberg, and Christoph Hochhäusler. The latter two are also key figures of the Berlin School and editors of the influential film journal *Revolver*, in which interviews with Ade have been featured.

When she first enrolled at the HFF in 1998, Ade did so to study production, only to switch into directing during her second year, yet she never lost sight of the significance the producer plays in shaping every aspect of a film. Indeed, her role as producer is as significant for her overall career as directing and writing are. During her second year at the HFF, Ade founded the production company Komplizen Film with fellow student Janine Jackowski (also from Karlsruhe), who produced Ade's graduation project and first feature, *The Forest for the Trees*. Jonas Dornbach joined the team in 2010, after serving as line producer on *Everybody Else*. In its more than twenty years of existence, Komplizen Film has made a name for itself among nonindustry filmmakers for promoting independent art cinema, with a proven track record of providing work opportunities to a broad range of artists, including many women and minority filmmakers. In an age of industry-driven productions, Komplizen Film promotes a sustainable mode of filmmaking based on transnational funding, often involving as partners the Austrian production company coop99, of which directors Barbara Albert and Jessica Hausner are important members.[13] Komplizen Film favors shared risks and collaboration over cutthroat individualism. "We produce local films for an international audience, films that take risks," the company's website explains. "We work with filmmakers distinguished by a unique signature and believe in long-term cooperation with our directors and production partners."[14]

In recent years, the company's success has been widely acknowledged. Among the most prestigious honors were the 2015 DEFA-Stiftung Award for outstanding accomplishments in German cinema, and, in 2019, the Best Producer Award at Locarno Film Festival. To date, Komplizen Film's website lists thirty-one completed features, among them those by Berlin School directors Benjamin Heisenberg, Ulrich Köhler, and Valeska Grisebach; other German directors include Sonja Heiss (with four features to date), Vanessa Hopp and Anna Sofie Hartmann. Top European filmmakers include Miguel Gomes (Portugal), Corneliu Porumboiu and Radu Jude (both from Romania), Emin Alper (Turkey), and Jasmila Žbanić (Bosnia). Since 2018, the company has also gone beyond Europe to team up with Nadav Lapid (Israel), Hajooj (Sudan), and Maya Da-Rin (Brazil), and a collaboration with Lisandro Alonso (Argentina) is in the works. Komplizen Film has, of course, produced all of Ade's own features. Apart from *Toni Erdmann*, the company's biggest critical and commercial success to date is the Academy Award winner *Una mujer fantástica* (*A Fantastic Woman*) by Chilean director Sebastián Lelio.

Since Ade assumes the role of producer, writer, and director and actively participates in the editing process and the distribution of her films, she commands an extraordinary degree of control over her works, which affords her the luxury of being able to pay attention to detail. This artisanal mode of filmmaking requires a long maturation process, which clearly sets Komplizen Film at odds with the demands of the global film industry. In an interview with Mark Peranson, Ade has commented that writing the script for *Toni Erdmann* took almost two years, while editing more than one hundred hours of footage took another eighteen months. And, she added, "I became a mother twice during all of that."[15] Negotiating these challenges has become a trademark of Ade's company. As a film that carefully tallies the fallout from the neoliberal economy, *Toni Erdmann* can be seen as a highly self-reflexive commentary on this process. Just like its shaggy titular hero, the film adopts the absurd disguise of a German comedy to pose serious questions about tragic topics that include death, the loneliness of the modern businesswoman, and the meaning of life, all the while reaching global audiences and tapping into markets usually beyond reach for such niche productions.

Learning from Andy Kaufman

When *Toni Erdmann* premiered at Cannes, one of the main talking points in Anglo-American reviews was that the film was a German comedy. Even though many critics were quick to add that the film was not a *pure* comedy, this hook had been planted and was then employed, to great success, in advertising campaigns and promotional materials. While this choice of genre would hardly have been worth emphasizing in, say, a French or Italian film, it was noteworthy here, because outside of Germany the terms "German" and "comedy" are usually considered mutually exclusive. It was no surprise, then, that one of the first questions Ade had to field during the festival concerned the origins of her sense of humor. What was a surprise, however, was Ade's acknowledgement of American standup comedian and performance artist Andy Kaufman as the main inspiration for the pranks of the father figure.[16] As the director explained, "it took four weeks to Google everything about Andy Kaufman," clearly committing to the same kind of thorough research that she also did regarding the real-life business woman that informed Sandra Hüller's role and to scouting the locations frequented by the Bucharest professional elite.[17]

Hardly known outside his native country, Kaufman's brand of humor is widely considered to break with norms and genres. His career began in the 1970s with appearances at New York comedy clubs, where he performed as Foreign Man, a heavy-accented stranger with a meek voice from "Caspiar," a fictional island in the Caspian Sea. Reviewing the show in 1974, the *New York Times* critic Richard F. Shepard described Kaufman as a "brilliantly funny performer . . . a comedian who defies categorization."[18] This persona was then morphed into Latka Gravas on the widely popular US television sitcom *Taxi*, which ran from 1978 to 1983. The Latka character was given a multiple personality disorder in order to accommodate Kaufman's desire to perform numerous characters. Arguably Kaufman's best-known creation, though, is Tony Clifton, a Las Vegas-style lounge singer who abuses and offends his audience. (Toni Erdmann's name pays direct homage to both this character and its inventor.) By sometimes having his brother or another person perform as Clifton, Kaufman intentionally muddled Clifton's identity, even claiming that he was a different person altogether, intent on abusing Kaufman's good name. As "Inter Gender Wrestling-Champion of the World," Kaufman next began wrestling women on television, using characters invented by professional wrestlers but often employing mean or abusive conduct.[19] In all of his many incarnations, Kaufman profoundly—and uncomfortably—blurred

Layered identities: Andy Kaufman as Caspiar doing Elvis Presley. From the Johnny Carson Show, 1977: https://www.youtube.com/watch?v=9kpBzUQHYtM.

the line between what is funny and what is not. Commenting that "Kaufman was very radical in how he created his roles," Ade speaks for the majority of people who knew him, though not all of them shared her admiration.[20] For younger generations, Kaufman, who died in 1984 at the age of thirty-five, is now known mostly for being celebrated in R.E.M.'s song, "Man on the Moon" (1992). His story was brought to the screen in Miloš Forman's eponymous 1999 biopic, starring Jim Carrey as Kaufman.[21] For the majority of people who did know him, he remains someone they simply did not get.

Kaufman's appearance on the David Letterman show in October 1980 is legendary; he made the seasoned late-night host visibly ill at ease with a runny nose and his refusal to say much. At a loss for words, Letterman rushed Kaufman to perform his act, where, affecting a complete lack of self-confidence, he gave a monosyllabic monologue about his failed marriage, explicitly asking people not to laugh. Refusing to follow the conventional pattern of such confessional moments, Kaufman did not end on a more hopeful and conciliatory note but instead begged audience members for spare change, before being escorted off stage by security. Letterman sarcastically commented on his exit, accompanied by a close-up of the EXIT sign, by saying, "always a pleasure to have the young talent on the show." Kaufman's radical antiperformance, and his remarkable consistency in staying in character until he was marched out of the studio, snubbing the audience and refusing to deliver what they craved, made them swallow their laughter and their empathy.[22]

Being able to walk this very fine line, and frequently crossing it, is what mattered for Peter Simonischek's performance of Winfried as Toni. The businessman and coach with a "special focus on life" is by turns ludicrous, outrageous, and even sadistic, but ultimately also deeply caring and human. The crucial difference between this character and Andy Kaufman's (or those of most other comedians and dilettante pranksters, for that matter) is that Toni Erdmann's antics are fueled by desperation.[23] Being silly or irreverent is a matter

"Hello, my name is Toni Erdmann."

of life or death for Ines's father, even if the stakes remain unclear to her (at least at first). This fine line, too, needed to be conveyed through Simonischek's performance. As Ade notes, the actor was never allowed to ham it up too much, because it was never just fun that propelled Toni Erdmann's pranks but always something existential.[24] In contrast to Kaufman's performances, then, "Ade's execution," Andrew Lapin notes, "is far more emotionally textured."[25]

In a promotional interview created for the German DVD release of *Toni Erdmann*, Simonischek cited two other role models that went into Winfried's alter ego: "Toni Erdmann has something of Helge Schneider as well as of Mick Jagger. He's a bit of a pop star."[26] While Toni's shaggy hair and eagerness to claim center stage may recall the frontman of the Rolling Stones (including Jagger's desire to act younger than his actual age), so does the blonde mane of Schneider, a multitalented artist with a cultlike following in Germany (apart from being a comedian, he is also an accomplished jazz musician, film and theater director, actor, and novelist). Yet while Toni Erdmann shares Schneider's talent for parody and improvisation,

Schneider's crude humor and horseplay mentality seem a bit of a stretch for the more refined business coach. Sometimes also cited as a potential influence—and closer to Winfried's own generation—is Loriot (the pseudonym of Vicco von Bülow, 1923–2011), a widely popular and beloved German comedian, cartoonist, actor, director, and writer, whose sense of humor often revolves around conflicts between ordinary people trying to hold onto their dignity in absurd and challenging everyday scenarios.[27] While *Toni Erdmann* shares Loriot's talent for improvisation, neither dignity nor stoicism is any of his concern.

On the whole, then, German comedians in particular, and German traditions of humor in general, did not have a great impact on Ade's film. This is surprising, given that German film comedy enjoys a vibrant tradition that harks back to the Weimar Republic and that even endured in films made during the Third Reich, the immediate, dire postwar years, and in state-controlled East German cinema. Indeed, comedies have rarely been out of favor with German audiences; still today, comedy is by far the most successful domestic genre when it comes to the box office, and the only one capable of challenging the dominance of Hollywood blockbusters on the German market. That said, even among the most popular titles only few were able to make inroads abroad; *Good Bye, Lenin* (Wolfgang Becker, 2003) is one such rare exception. What is more, *Toni Erdmann* was not the most commercially successful 2016 film in Germany by a long shot; that honor fell to *Willkommen bei den Hartmanns* (*Welcome to Germany*) by Simon Verhoeven, a refugee comedy that grossed over $20 million, with Ade's film landing in a distant fortieth place.

While *Toni Erdmann*'s use of comedy stands out among mainstream German cinema, it is also a bit of an outlier among films of the Berlin School, which have stayed away from comedies (with the single exception of *Über-Ich und Du* [*Superegos*], a 2014 film directed by Benjamin Heisenberg and produced by Komplizen Film). Indeed, because of its use of comedy, Ade's film came under attack from her Berlin School colleague Christoph Hochhäusler (a rare case of friendly fire, which I will address below). Yet Ade's interest in comedy should not be all that surprising. As a bodily genre, comedy allows directors to explore mixed or competing affects, including embarrassment and shame, which are crucial to all of Ade's films. *Toni Erdmann*'s use of physical comedy and its emphasis on the body explore discomfort in complex and contradictory ways. The insecurity of her protagonists—whether Melanie, Gitti, or Ines—clearly resonates with viewers. And unlike other Berlin School films, in which silence often reigns supreme (Thomas Arslan's early films or Angela Schanelec's *Marseille* come to mind), all of Ade's feature are dialogue-heavy and dialogue-driven, with *Toni Erdmann* moving close to situational comedy. Emphasizing the structural affinities of all three of Ade's features to sitcoms, Muriel Cormican has called them "situation tragedies," clearly recognizing that laughing about someone else comes at a price and is never innocent.[28]

The uniqueness of Ade's use of comedy might be best illustrated by comparing it to the films of Doris Dörrie, Ade's erstwhile teacher at the HFF and one of the commercially most successful German directors of the last decades. While Ade claims to have few recollections of the directing classes she took with Dörrie at Munich, she clearly studied Dörrie's films well, as two examples will illustrate. The opening scene of Ade's film, which first introduces the Toni Erdmann character, in a bathrobe and banana in hand, clearly quotes from Doris Dörrie's breakout success *Männer. . . (Men. . .)* (1985), as does the Kukeri costume worn by Winfried at Ines's naked birthday reception. Both getups reference a gorilla mask, used by Dörrie as a significant instrument of deceit in *Men. . .*, which revolves around a classic love triangle: the successful designer Julius cheats on his wife Paula with one of his secretaries. When he learns that Paula, too, has taken a lover—the penniless freelance artist and bon vivant Stefan—he goes on an elaborate mission to win her back. Posing as

"Daniel," he moves in with Stefan, befriends him, and slowly instills in him professional ambition and a taste for the good life, ultimately turning him into a carbon copy of himself and thereby achieving the desired outcome that Paula loses interest in Stefan. At a crucial point in the film, Paula comes to visit Stefan and, afraid to blow his cover, Julius dons a bathrobe and the above-noted gorilla mask beneath which he, like Winfried in his Kukeri costume, remains completely silent, while his anarchic role-play disrupts the romantic setting. For its advertising campaign, the film frequently used the stand-alone image of a banana as a symbol for Julius's monkey business.

A second film by Dörrie to which *Toni Erdmann* has a certain structural affinity is *Kirschblüten—Hanami* (*Cherry Blossoms*) (2008), which centers on the aging and lonely Rudi. After suddenly losing his wife, Rudi decides to travel to Japan, a country that had always fascinated her but that she never had a chance to visit. While there, Rudi tries to reconnect with his estranged son, but he is rebuffed as the son's career keeps him too busy to find time for the father. With the help of a woman that he befriends, Rudi travels to Mount Fuji—which had been a life-long dream of his wife—where, after several foggy days, he awakens one night to discover the moonlit mountain in plain sight. Painting his face and donning his wife's kimono, he slips away and dances at the mountain's foot before he collapses and passes away. The overtly ambitious estranged offspring, the lonely father, and the ubiquitous presence of death—it's all there. Yet as these snapshot synopses may suggest, both these Dörrie films, and the vast majority of her features, establish clear binary oppositions with one-dimensional and predictable characters, and the experience of conflict is neatly resolved at the film's end, whether through compromise, improbable change, or sudden death. As Heinz Drügh has observed, in contrast to Dörrie's *Men. . .*, "*Toni Erdmann* knows that it would be too simplistic and trite to employ a model of comedy in which all those who are stubborn become enlightened, those who are uptight become relaxed, and where the main basic conflict simply disappears at the end"—a verdict that applies in equal measure to *Cherry Blossoms*.[29]

Yet Doris Dörrie's films are important to consider here not only for their superficial similarities but because the influential model of filmmaking Dörrie first introduced holds sway until today and is anathema to Berlin School filmmakers. While widely celebrated as a surprise success, it is no accident that *Men*. . . hit the screens in 1986: not only did the film follow on the heels of the demise of the New German Cinema, which is widely held to have died when Fassbinder died, in 1982, but *Men*. . . is clearly the one film that both pronounced and cemented its death. "More than any German film of the 1980s," Eric Rentschler has claimed, *Men*. . . "articulated a generation's deep disdain for the dreams of 1968 about a better life and an alternative existence. . . . Its crucial passages focus on the formation of identity as an exercise in the manipulation of images. Julius remakes Stefan, attiring him in a new wardrobe, redoing his hair, giving him lessons in managerial style, showing him how to gaze, how to negotiate, how to make commercial illustrations more appealing by throwing in a slight touch of the unconventional."[30] In short, Julius converts Stefan to the gospel of neoliberalism that was starting to take hold in German minds and businesses at that precise time. *Men*. . . paved a way for a whole slew of commercially successful films that would dominate the 1990s, most of them (romantic) comedies. Together, they make up what Rentschler has labeled the German cinema of consensus—a body of films that is predominantly bland, provincial, and harmless, often featuring protagonists in their mid-thirties and the growing pains they experience as they transition from a carefree bohemian student life into professional careers and long-term relationships. The identity crises that these protagonists undergo, adds Rentschler, are "in fact pseudo-crises, for they have no depth of despair, no true suffering, no real joy."[31]

While Ines may share some of this generation's rebuke of the 1968ers (as we will see in more detail below), the way Ade chooses to tell that story is decidedly at odds with the superficial conventions of the feel-good movies and new age harmonies advocated by Dörrie and her epigones. Resurrecting a commitment to the *Autorenfilm* and to the independent cinema that Dörrie had made it her mission to bury, Ade and her Berlin School colleagues can be seen as heirs of the New German Cinema, underscored by the movements' recognition abroad and its success at international festivals—a recognition that, with a few exceptions, had not existed since the mid-1980s.[32]

"I don't know much about German comedies," Maren Ade has told an interviewer. "I think most of the comedies that are made try to copy American comedies, maybe, and then you get a strange mixture that doesn't work anymore."[33] The humor of *Toni Erdmann* works precisely because Maren Ade stays away from the shallow models that dominate German productions. Beyond Andy Kaufman, two more influential artists need to be mentioned here: Ernst Lubitsch and Billy Wilder. While the Berliner Lubitsch and the Austrian Wilder began their remarkable careers in the Weimar film industry, they did not develop the sense of humor that made them famous until they joined the Hollywood studios, making their "accented" take on life particularly fertile ground for inspiration.[34] Ade, the German journalist Katja Nicodemus has asserted, is indebted "to Wilder and Lubitsch because she's closer to that deep humanism—the masquerades, the salaciousness, the wit, the social critique of those comedies, in a subconscious way."[35] A case in point is Billy Wilder's *The Apartment* (1960), a moving romantic comedy that revolves around C. C. Baxter (Jack Lemmon), an office climber, and elevator girl Fran Kubelik (Shirley MacLaine). Here Lemmon plays a lowly insurance company clerk whose strategy for career advancement involves subletting his apartment by the hour for his supervisors' extramarital trysts, in exchange for a higher rung on the office ladder. His neighbor, the inquisitive Dr. Dreyfus, mistakenly attributes the sex and booze flowing freely next door to Baxter's own addiction to vice and urges him to better his ways:

"Be a Mensch, Baxter, you know, a human being." When he falls hard for Fran, Baxter finally stands up to his boss, and in losing his job he wins the girl—a clear indication that he has heeded doctor's orders. While *The Apartment* comes closer to the happy ending that *Toni Erdmann* clearly eschews, Wilder's unsettling portrayal of assembly-line, white-collar workers offers a scathing satire of a Fordist economy that makes for an instructive comparison to the post-Fordist Romania of today that is portrayed in Ade's film, as well as to the corporate types it creates. While both workplaces are infused with a sense of despair and loneliness that pervades all aspects of public and private life, remaining human in today's new economy proves an even bigger challenge than in the administered world of the late 1950s. Suffice it to say that Baxter's efforts to win the attention (and the heart) of Miss Kubelik, while nurturing her back to life after a suicide attempt, succeed partly because of a uniquely prepared dish of spaghetti, something Winfried also tries on his daughter, but in vain.[36]

"I Like Countries with a Middle Class"

Thus comments Natalja Henneberg, the Russian wife of Ines's top client, on her life in Frankfurt, where the couple has a second home. There is a certain nostalgic ring to Natalja's affection for places with a middle class. In Romania, as well as in her native Russia, the middle class has long ceased to exist (if it had ever even gained a foothold), as decades of state-ruled socialism have been replaced by salvage capitalism. The remark is both revealing and deeply ironic. Most obviously, it puts the finger on the paradox that businessmen like Natalja's husband, an avatar of the new economy, are busy doing away with the very form of existence that she cherishes. Some twenty years his junior, Natalja is a trophy wife for whom marriage likely meant a life in material comfort, using her good looks to bridge an income gap that most of her fellow countrymen will never close.

And I would like to buy some presents.

Natalja, the trophy wife.

Ines's snippy observation of Henneberg's wife as "very Russian, very skinny, very blond" suggests as much (and, for good measure, adds a revealing slur). Yet, if the generational transition between Ines and her father is any indication, the kind of middle class exemplified by bourgeois Winfried also appears headed for extinction, making Natalja's comment even more poignant.

What a society without a middle class looks like is on display in almost every scene in *Toni Erdmann*. Its main players are consultants, CEOs, and real estate agents, shuffling between meetings, building "a business case," and advising on how to modernize (i.e., downsize) a moribund conglomerate. Conspicuous consumption is on display in Europe's largest mall and in five-star hotels with fancy bars and restaurants, as well as in nightclubs where stressful jobs are palliated through alcohol and designer drugs. Glitzy facades, peopled with hostesses and receptionists dressed to the hilt, spill over into drab office suites—the symptomatic spaces of the post-Fordist society. Ines's apartment, luxurious but devoid of any personal touch, is a place she dwells in but does not really inhabit, oozing a form of neglect that Winfried captures when he takes a picture of a withered flower.

Winfried captures signs of neglect in Ines's apartment.

The gap between the haves and the have-nots is widening fast. The Romanian economy is praised by the American ambassador as offering "significant opportunities to American businesses with products, services, or technologies that either meet growing private demand or contribute to the country's development priorities," while Henneberg explains the advantages the country holds for West Europeans: "The sea is very close, there are good French private schools—Romania is a lot better than its reputation." Yet few Romanians have the money to shop for the mostly imported products on display at the Bucharest mall—unlike their counterparts in Western societies—which are geared toward the middle class. The mall's very exclusivity makes it the capitalist counterpart of Nicolae Ceaușescu's enormous Palace of the Parliament or Casa Poporului (the people's palace).

As Ines explains, the mall is actually "more Romanian than the Palace," because it says more about contemporary Romania than the remnants of the dictator's personality cult do. Not unlike in the federal republic of the 1950s, the building of a competitive economy, fueled by foreign money, takes priority over working through the

Only glimpsed briefly through the windshield, the monumental Casa Poporului.

More Romanian than the palace: the mall of Bucharest.

trauma inflicted by a totalitarian regime. Making the country a player in the expanded European Union is clearly an important political goal, much like aligning West Germany's postwar politics with those of NATO.

As a result of this widening gap, a growing precariat confronts a small group of quick, adaptable learners. At Henneberg's prompting, Ines praises Romania's corporate culture and work mentality by emphasizing that the new generation has international degrees and speaks several languages, while a Romanian colleague injects that "they don't understand Romania any more. They are faster than the rest of the country. They don't want to stay here." This gap between the mobile, affluent class and those locked in time and place is most succinctly captured by a cut-away shot from the multinational office building, where Ines has just concluded her presentation (on the necessity of outsourcing), to an abutting ramshackle settlement. Maren Ade has explained that this shot, which lasts almost twenty seconds, was not in the script. "I decided on the spot [to include it] because it's exactly the view from the building."[37] As Andrew Lapin has aptly noted, this "sly, devastating shot reveals that Romania's business class has built itself on the backs of the poor."[38] As this shot also makes clear, the hub of globalization is actually an island within a country that is predominantly premodern, bypassed not only by the developments following the joining of the European Union but also by decades of socialist modernization—a time lag rendered tangible when Ines and Winfried visit a moribund oil production plant outside the city.

Toni Erdmann "constitutes a landmark in the cinematic representation of neoliberalism," Hester Baer has rightly claimed.[39] Indeed, the neoliberal economy has been a main paradigm in understanding the cinema of the Berlin School.[40] During the movement's first years, many films were devoted to exploring the unequal economic developments in East and West Germany over the decade and a half following the fall of the Berlin Wall. Avoiding the topic-related kind of filmmaking that informs many German films about the Third Reich, the Stasi, or the Red Army terrorists of the 1970s, Berlin School films have opted for taking a long view to fathom the human casualties, among them the privatization of

The global meets the local: Bucharest's asynchronous synchronicities.

social services and the eradication of a social safety net, in particular by exploring the subtle fault lines between East and West. "These films use extreme precision to achieve ambiguous, sometimes deeply strange effects," Dennis Lim has remarked. "They insist on an engagement with the real world, though often through a hyperreal clarity that is itself a kind of stylization."[41]

The director most consistently concerned with honing in on this geoeconomic dichotomy is Christian Petzold—most notably, in *Yella* (2007), *Jerichow* (2008), and *Dreileben: Etwas Besseres als den Tod* (*Dreileben: Beats Being Dead*) (2011). A crucial scene from *Yella* revolves around the title character, a woman from the former East who has hopes of finding a better future in the West. She is coached by her new boss, Philipp, a young West German venture capitalist, on how to behave in business negotiations by showing her the so-called broker pose—hands folded behind the head, elbows raised—which he picked up, he admits, "from crappy Grisham movies." Even though he concedes that the whole thing looks phony, he asserts that it works well. Together with instructions about body language, the direction of her gaze, and when to whisper nonsense into his ear, the pose is one of several precise cues that Phillip impresses on his new recruit, which, taken together, symbolize what Petzold has called "the transformative bodies of neoliberalism."[42] Like *Toni Erdmann*, this scene, as well as Petzold's entire film, lays bare the many ironic layers of performing and performance in the new economy.[43] Indeed, making the neoliberal visible—finding new forms of cinematic expressions to make largely invisible or seemingly natural processes comprehensible —is at the core of these films by Ade and Petzold, as well as the Berlin School cinema more generally.

While Petzold's films can be said to be about faded borders—those that have disappeared as political entities but not as barriers controlling access to the good life—Christoph Hochhäusler's debut feature *Milchwald* (*This Very Moment*) (2003) fathoms the complex social and psychological makeup of the Polish borderlands in the summer preceding that country's accession to the European Union. The film invokes the genre of the fairy tale to debunk German stereotypes of the region as a hotbed of prostitution, car theft, and organized crime, casting it instead as a place of enchantment that both invites and challenges German projections of "Polishness." Whereas Petzold is interested in exposing the fissures that have opened up because of the asynchronous temporalities and spaces that divide West and East Germany, Hochhäusler creates a speculative scenario of what the Eastern expansion of the European Union might mean.

The full impact of that expansion comes under scrutiny not only in *Toni Erdmann* but also in Valeska Grisebach's *Western*, set on the border between Bulgaria and Greece and revolving around a German construction crew building a hydraulic pump.[44] It is a companion piece of sorts to Ade's last feature—and a critically acclaimed film in its own right. The two films' proximity is not entirely surprising, as Ade and Grisebach have been close collaborators over many years, serving as each other's script advisors and interlocutors, and Komplizen Film also produced *Western*.[45] As Grisebach's title indicates, her film invokes the narrative conventions and iconography of that most American of film genres while deliberately withholding on that promise. Eschewing action and psychological motivation, *Western* explores notions of foreignness and male rivalry through a meandering, slow-moving, and unpredictable narrative, employing a visual style that is observational and subtle in its probing of cultural difference. Both *Western* and *Toni Erdmann* pay close attention to the language of the respective class that they depict, be it the male jargon and broad Berlin dialect of the construction workers or the vacuous Denglish corporate speak of the new entrepreneurs. And both films cast the business of their respective protagonists as quasi-colonial encounters, euphemistically labeled an investment in the former socialist states, the beneficiaries of which will not be the Bulgarian or Romanian villagers but people in Berlin or elsewhere. As Grisebach has noted, her work brigade embodies "a colonial attitude," summarized neatly in the words of the foreman who explains, "wir bringen hier Infrastruktur mit 'rin" (we're introducing infrastructure here) as a way of justifying secretly diverting water from a local village and negatively impacting the environment.[46]

The genres loosely employed by Grisebach, Hochhäusler, and Petzold—the western, the fairy tale, and horror, respectively—are exemplary of the Berlin School's creative use of genre. *Toni Erdmann* is unique within this group for exposing the fallout of the new economy under the cover of comedy, only to strike a less reconciliatory tone. In contrast to more mainstream films about globalization, the new economy is not a strawman target represented by stereotypes in suits. And contrary to, say, many Ken Loach films—particularly *Sorry We Missed You* (2019) or *I, Daniel Blake* (2016) (the film, incidentally, that beat *Toni Erdmann* for the Palme d'Or)—which are all about empathy for the plight of the small people and a celebration of their dignity, Ade is interested in both sides of the story. She does this not only by shifting the main perspective from Winfried to Ines halfway through the film but also by paying careful attention to the contradictions that govern their respective views and behavior.

A throwaway scene at the Bucharest mall provides a good example of how delicately *Toni Erdmann* touches on these contradictions. By then, viewers have already witnessed how Winfried's sudden intrusion into Ines's life shines a harsh light on the hollow center of the new economy. At the mall we realize that his views, which were formed before the world became globalized, are not without their own inconsistencies. When Winfried meets Ines as she is wrapping up shopping with Natalja, he's carrying a Lidl bag (with groceries for the spaghetti dinner he will later cook for her, so as to inaugurate the new cheese grater, his birthday present to her). The business model of this discount grocery store, which has perfected the neoliberal dictates that Ines advocates, has allowed the chain to establish itself all over Europe and the East Coast of the United States. Yet this success has brought with it closer scrutiny and allegations of ruthlessly exploiting its monopoly position and abusing government subsidies, thus distorting true competition—allegations of which Winfried seems unaware. This disconnect between a consumer's individual advantage and the larger social imbalance is the very blind spot on which Ines puts her finger when she returns with Winfried

The ubiquity of Lidl.

after inspecting the oil rig. "In every step you make I can tell you your economic connection to these people," she lectures him. "Your 'green' attitude won't help you." In their high-stakes game of poking holes into each other's philosophy of life, Ines clearly scores a point here. On a more personal scale this direct link between Winfried's life and the Romanians is also evident in Germany (though it is apparently unnoticed by Winfried). Judging by her name and accent, Mrs. Rodica, his mother's aide, is from Romania and part of a predominantly East European workforce that serves as housekeepers and caretakers for Germany's aging population, making Winfried and his family the direct beneficiaries of unequal economies.

The End(s) of Sleep

The first time we meet Ines is when Winfried comes to visit Renate, at whose home in Aachen Ines has just arrived from Bucharest. "The flight was okay?," he asks his ex-wife, while they observe their daughter answering a call on the veranda. "Yes," replies Renate, "she is tired." As we get to know Ines better, we realize that what looks like mere travel-related fatigue is a serious and recurring issue. Twice she falls asleep—once when she is in the car with her father (on the way to and from the oil plant that they are inspecting) and, most dramatically, deep sleep overcomes her when she takes a predinner nap and wakes up the next morning, thereby missing an important meeting with Henneberg. Ines's sleep deprivation is of course not just an individual problem but indeed a chronic symptom for young business executives like her.

The significance of sleep, or more precisely the lack thereof, in today's neoliberal society is the subject of a pair of fascinating studies by two leading contemporary thinkers, Jonathan Crary, an American art critic, and the German-Korean philosopher Bjung-Chul Han. Both writers agree that the reduction of sleep is the direct result of the dramatically increased efficiency of cycles of production,

Repeatedly, sleep overcomes Ines at the wrong moment.

circulation, and consumption of goods and information. Never before have working people been under greater pressure to conform to the demands of markets and networks. Today's hyperconnectedness (which in most places increased even more during the COVID-19 pandemic), has resulted in a blurring of work time and nonwork time and profoundly altered our perception and experience of time. Tellingly, Ines's appointment with Henneberg, which she overslept but during which she was meant to show him and his wife the nightlife of Bucharest, was scheduled for midnight—that is, long after "regular hours."

For Crary, sleep becomes not only a luxury but an active form of resistance in this new social environment. Because of its profound uselessness and intrinsic passivity, "sleep will always collide with the demands of a 24/7 universe. The huge portion of our lives that we spend asleep, freed from the morass of simulated needs, subsists as one of the great human affronts to the voraciousness of contemporary capitalism."[47] By understanding the capitalist order as the Other that subdues us, Crary invokes traditional leftist views. The digital world's promise of a newfound freedom—namely, the ability to work from anywhere at any time—is for him a sign of increasing enslavement. While Byung-Chul Han agrees with much of what Crary says about the impact of neoliberalism, he contends that the change from a postindustrial society to our digital age has altered the very experience of subjectivity and the relationship between self and other. In his influential study, *Müdigkeitsgesellschaft* (translated as *Burnout Society*, even though a more literal rendition would be fatigue society or tiredness society), Han takes the phenomenon of chronic fatigue as a symptom of a widespread problem among advanced Western societies. In the age of neoliberalism, capitalism is no longer tough, as Crary asserts, but seductive. It has produced what Han calls the achievement subject—a form of subjectivity that is no longer liable to external control. Instead, achievement subjects have been conditioned to exploit themselves.[48]

Like Crary, Han asserts that private life and the very notion of privacy are crumbling in the digital age. Yet this is primarily the case because the self is now virtual, for all to be seen, commented on, "liked." Today's psychopolitics, Han contends, no longer works through coercion. Rather than forbidding and depriving, performance is all about being pleasing and fulfilling; instead of making people compliant, psychopolitics makes them dependent. Slogans such as "Yes we can," and "Just do it"—used in Nike commercials, in the Obama presidential campaign, and for numerous protests throughout Latin American countries, to give just a sampling—are not, according to Han, empowering, because they imply "Yes, we should." We have volunteered to succumb to the pressure of achieving, Han contends; we are slaves to the culture of positivity. The state of exhaustion is the result of an incessant compulsion to perform. It is telling that we see Ines fall asleep only in the presence of her father; with him, it seems, she can let her guard down. While his visit clearly irritates her, it is also strangely soothing—an experience that reaches its climax when she embraces him in his Kukeri costume, giving him a bear hug that provides a (temporary) release not only from the tension brought on by his visit but more generally from the demands of her career. Lastly, the scene also has a great impact on the affective economy of the spectator.

For Han, today's capitalism is no longer founded on exploitation by the Other but by the self—as our own entrepreneurs, we self-coerce for maximum output. "Yes we can" and "Just do it" suggest that there are no limits to what we can achieve; we just need to try harder. These ethics of self-improvement have clearly been internalized by Ines and her colleagues. A very telling indicator of her quest to maximize personal output is her engagement of a personal coach. A coach's job is to fine-tune performance for better efficiency. As such, a coach is essentially an amplified and individualized version of self-help books (the script describes Winfried discovering a charisma guide on Ines's bookshelf), self-help groups, performance enhancing food supplements and drugs (including sleep suppressant and sleeping pills, depending on current need), and neuroenhancers. During a Skype conversation with her coach Leopold (Nicolas Wackerbarth), Ines discusses working on her body language. Tellingly, he advises her to use identification with the other as "tool

Advice from the coach: Not too much empathy, please!

[in English in the original] that you have to be able to put aside" (as the script has it).

Empathy, Leopold implies, can clearly be counterproductive if the self is to be the main focus. While Leopold knows all about the business world, he clearly positions himself at its margins. On Ines's laptop screen, we see him seated outside some Alpine lodge and wearing local garb. "Coaches," Heinz Drügh observes, "have to create a position outside or opposed to the mainstream, whether through athleticism or affinity to nature, which suggest that you're dealing with an artist."[49] In the business world, coaches are often referred to as gurus—people whose advice one is willing to accept on faith only. (Included in the script but not the film is Ines's line, "a lot of managers have strange gurus," with which she defends her father when her friend Steph mocks Toni's disgusting table manners.)

It makes perfect sense, then, that this is the profession that Toni Erdmann claims to occupy when he introduces himself to a surprised Steph and Tatjana during their girls' night out with Ines. On the one hand, the necessity for a coach is probably as incomprehensible to Winfried as is Anca's understanding of performance; for him, it embodies everything that's wrong with Ines's professional develop-ment and the world in which she circulates. At the same time, he clearly picks up on the nonconformist nature of this profession, which attracts him. Even though he is not privy to Ines's Skype conversation with her coach, his own over-the-top outfit is just an exaggerated version of Leopold's garb. And while Toni is not successful in his impersonation of the German ambassador (the woman he tries to fool, his new acquaintance Flavia, lets on that she knows the real ambassador), his claim to be the consultant and coach of Romanian tennis legend and business magnate Ion Țiriac cannot entirely be ruled out. (Țiriac has a brief cameo in the scene in which Ines first introduces her father to Henneberg.)[50] The markers defining a coach are murky enough to possibly include someone like Toni, and the risk of slighting a *real* coach, especially one with such a powerful client,

In the shot for only a nanosecond: the iconoclastic Ion Ţiriac.

is simply too big. As a result, Toni's bluff is constantly suspected by those around him, but it can never really be called.

Ines's obsession with performance is also an obsession with performing her gender "right," so as to pass muster with her male peers. Asking her coach for feedback on her body language is a thinly veiled plea to eradicate signs of "female" weakness or vulnerability. Her preoccupation with looks—both her own and those of her protégé Anca, whom she instructs about how to cover the blood stain on her blouse with her hair—is noteworthy here, because the threat that her father poses is first and foremost directed at her appearance. He literally imprints himself twice on her immaculate outfit—first by smudging his stage makeup on her blazer in Aachen and then, more indirectly, by causing her to stub her toe when she puts away his hideaway bed, which in turn will soil her blouse. In a more general sense, Toni's antics challenge Ines's efforts to appear to be in control, an appearance that is clearly gendered as male. The fact that gender can be performed "incorrectly" is an indication that, contrary to its promise of equality, mobility, and self-empowerment, the neoliberal workplace is saturated with traditional gender bias and the remnants of patriarchy and male entitlement. Indeed, neoliberalism is a highly gendered cultural formation (a subject on which both Crary and Han remain silent, as do other influential thinkers such as David Harvey and Stuart Hall).[51]

In an interview given at Cannes, just prior to the premiere of *Toni Erdmann*, Maren Ade stated that she did not set out to make a film about sexism in the workplace but simply strove to make a realistic film.[52] Yet even casual viewers cannot overlook how overtly sexist behavior shapes Ines's everyday job experience (it must be noted, however, that, she ultimately fights back against the sexism, and in highly creative ways). We notice that at social events the businessmen surrounding Ines are more willing to talk to the bizarre Toni Erdmann than to her. Her client Henneberg does not think twice about "volunteering" Ines to take his wife shopping or showing them Bucharest's nightlife. Imposing even further on her privacy, her boss Gerald tells Tim to advise her not to have too much sex, so as not to lose "her bite." A further twist in the film's running joke about teeth, this association between teeth and the prowess of a (male) predator is reinforced through Gerald's praise—"you're an animal!"—following her successful case presentation to Henneberg and the Romanian business associates. The visual composition of that presentation clearly lays bare the objectification of Ines in the business world. Standing next to the screen, she, like the figures she presents, is there to be measured and calculated by the four businessmen who make up her audience. The scene is comprised of a series of shots taken from over Ines's shoulder to show the two pairs of men across from her, only briefly cutting to medium-shots of Ines,

Ines's business partners size up her data—and her.

who is struggling for composure as the business case she proposes comes under scrutiny from both sides.

Yet Ines also internalizes modes of male superiority. In her exchanges with Anca, Ines plays (male) top dog, nudging her assistant to improve her German (when the lingua franca in the business world is English) or to give her back her clean blouse in exchange for her own soiled garment. Anca's labor is invisible to Ines, who is unaware that her assistant has spent hours finding the right apartment for her. In an even more dramatic reversal of gender roles, Ines emasculates her partner Tim, by refusing to have sex with him and challenging him instead to masturbate on a petit four, which she then proceeds to eat, yet another allusion to her powerful bite.

Ines's unfulfilling sex life, slated into an upscale hotel, signals an emotional disconnect rather than a reignition of a relationship gone stale, and is of a piece with a lack of romance in Melanie's life and Gitti's complicated relationship with Chris in Ade's previous films, *The Forrest for the Tree* and *Everybody Else*. Michael Richardson has suggested that so many sexual encounters in Berlin School films are unerotic and squirm-inducing because both the protagonist(s) and the viewer share an experience of palpable discomfort, augmented by a mode of representation that refuses to employ the standard fare of "soft focus shots, montages of hands moving across writhing, glossy bodies, and smooth jazz soundtracks. . . . Bad sex is but the bodily manifestation of the social alienation that plagues the characters that populate Berlin School cinema."[53] The bad sex, the high-stress job, the existential loneliness of the modern businesswoman—all this builds up an overwhelming pressure that is released, in a series of ever-more outrageous scenes, in the final act of the film. The puncturing of Ines's throbbing toenail has shown us that Ines is not squeamish about achieving release, but nothing has prepared viewers for two extended scenes in which Ines revolts against her father's paternalistic behavior and the confines of the gendered new economy reach new heights.

Ines swallows the fruits of Tim's sexual labor.

Tough as nails: Ines has just punctured her infected toe

When Winfried urges Ines to accompany him to an Easter celebration at the home of Flavia, a new acquaintance of his, she reluctantly comes along. While Flavia is a bit surprised that Toni has taken her up on an invitation that was, at best, meant as a sympathetic gesture, she makes the surprise guests truly feel welcome. On seeing beautifully decorated Easter eggs, Winfried "volunteers" Ines, whom he has introduced as his assistant, Ms. Schnuck, for a lesson in traditional dyeing techniques. What follows is an excruciatingly long scene in which Ines, despite her resistance, is forced into practicing a delicate craft, much "like a burnout patient is coerced into deceleration therapy."[54] Having spotted an electric keyboard, Winfried next suggests that he and Ines perform a little song, as a token of gratitude to their host. Again, Ines is cornered by her father and cannot escape without potentially creating a scene. Striking a few cords and asking his daughter under his breath to play along, he introduces her as "the fabulous Whitney Schnuck." The ensuing karaoke performance of Whitney Houston's "Greatest Love of All," which prompted on-screen applause by the audience at the film's Cannes premiere, marks the climax in father and daughter's battle of performances—it will indeed be the last time the two will face off directly—creating an experience where viewers are no longer able to discern, as Lukas Foerster has it, whether "we're now watching a duel or a duet between actors."[55] During the three stanzas of the song, Ines displays a full repertoire of facial and bodily gestures, as she dramatically shifts from being offended and sulking to being defiant and triumphant, culminating in a final stanza in which she pulls out all the stops or engages in what Ade has termed a "fuck you!" gesture toward her father.[56] After the song, she looks at her father, briefly nods, and is out of the apartment almost before the applause begins.

While most commentators agree on the liberating force of the performance, they have also honed in on the contrast between a gesture of genuine liberation and the use of what they consider extraordinarily schlocky music. Lyrics such as, "I decided long ago / never to walk in anyone's shadow / I depend on me" just seemed too obviously sentimental to capture the subtle ruptures between Ines and her father.[57] Yet this opposition between the allegedly authentic

Channeling Whitney Houston, Whitney Schnuck lets it all hang out.

(Ines's defiance) and the inauthentic (the superficial lyrics) misses the point that the two are of a piece. In an illuminating commentary on Whitney Houston's 1985 official video of the song, Ivan Kreilkamp has pointed out the remarkable similarities between Ines's relationship with her father and that of the child prodigy Whitney Houston and her overbearing mother, which are on display in the official video for "Greatest Love of All." Both the mother-daughter plot of the video and Ines's issues with her father share the theme of a talented child and her hovering parent. The penultimate in a long line of extraordinary performances, Ines's rendition of "Greatest Love of All" is, according to Kreilkamp, "at once a show-stopping musical performance, and an antithesis—or parody? or inverting mimicry?—of the corporate performance style in which she is an expert. It feels like Ines's ironic but also partly-joyful abandonment of all the corporate proprieties that until now she has been carefully observing."[58]

If, as Whitney Schnuck, Ines bares her soul, at the reception in her apartment the next morning, she bares her skin. Repurposed from a birthday party into a team-building exercise, the remarkable naked brunch occasions Ines's most assertive and creative stance against the rule of patriarchy in the workspace. Following a garment malfunction just prior to the arrival of her guests, she welcomes her first visitor, Steph, in her underwear, only to strip completely by the time her next guest arrives. Not everybody participates, but Ines's boss does, because it is in the service of "team-building," while her assistant does too because she rationalizes it as a "challenge." While Ines literally dons her birthday suit, her father appears not in an Adam's costume but in the full-haired, gigantic Kukeri costume from Bulgarian carnival. In contrast to Toni Erdmann's gift of gab, the Kukeri remains completely silent throughout the ten-minute scene, relying instead on the power of *garb*. Showcasing that Ines shares her father's gene for punditry and improvisation, Ade here takes embarrassment to new heights. The scene is also a testament to the fact that the director knows physical comedy á la Lubitsch, where each time a door opens a new minidrama begins. When Gerald extends his birthday wishes, he hands Ines her present, and as he is at that point without the object with which he had covered his genitals, her "true" present is revealed, a moment of victory that rewards Ines's brave act.[59] To be sure, though, the naked brunch scene is not harmless fun. "This scene," Hester Baer has aptly noted, "makes visible the illusion of neutrality that characterizes neoliberal subjectivity and unmasks insecurity as the dominant contemporary structure of experience; with its send-up of 'team-building,' the naked brunch points specifically to the lack of social solidarity in Ines's life and in today's world more broadly."[60]

The brunch scene also rewrites the first celebration of Ines's birthday in Aachen, during which her performance as the dutiful daughter provided a preview of what she is capable of in the boardroom. In that first encounter, Winfried's entrance is a triple whammy: he arrives late; he is still wearing his skull make-up, which he promptly smudges on his daughter's business suit; and he brings no present.

Ines recoils from the strange intruder.

His appearance at the brunch, in contrast, *is* his present. For once, his getup completely obliterates his identity—Gerald assumes that under the costume is a paid performer whose shock value is meant to enhance the team-building experience—and his height shatters the frame, and, by implication, the confines of Ines's world. When Ines at last recognizes her father, a remarkable pursuit ensues that culminates with an emotional embrace in the park. Employing the sole traveling shot in the entire film, the camera captures the busy streets of Bucharest, for the first time conveying a sense of place as it follows the Kukeri passing curious bystanders. Its encounter with an uninhibited and curious girl recalls Frankenstein's monster meeting with a girl in James Whale's 1931 adaptation of the novel, as if two creatures from different worlds were coming into contact.[61] Finally, Ines catches up to the Kukeri and disappears into a hairy embrace while she exhales, "Papa." While Ines's lifestyle and affect model social distancing *avant la lettre* (including the sex with Tim), the Kukeri's bear hug occasions a rare moment in which father and daughter make physical, psychological, and emotional contact.

The bear hug, a rare moment of release and intimacy.

"What do you mean by 'happy'?"

If the emperor has no clothes, as the naked brunch scene succinctly reveals, any hierarchy built on appearances collapses. One could call Ines's undoing of male privilege a classic feminist move. Yet when Gerald, in a preceding scene, teases her about her feminist sensibilities being ruffled by a snide comment from Henneberg, she snappily responds, "If I were a feminist, I wouldn't deal with guys like you." We are left to wonder what the notion of feminism means to Ines. Does she consider it impossible to insist on a feminist stance in her workplace? When denied the promised move to Shanghai, she does *not* accept this slap in the face and takes a job in Singapore with a competitor—a clear sign of independence and self-confidence. And she is obviously well aware of her macho environment, as an earlier exchange with Tim indicates. Taken aback that Ines prefers to spend the evening with her girlfriends rather than with him, he teases her, "Frauengruppe?" (women's group), to which she retorts: "Exactly. We speak about a women's quota, sexual harassment, and other such things." When dealing with men like Gerald and Tim,

Ines's replies suggest, humor might get you further than head-on confrontation.

Ines's reservations about the label *feminist* here echo Maren Ade's own. Reflecting on her studies at the University of Television and Film in Munich, Ade has explained that the statement "I am feminist" was considered uncool at the time: "I would have associated it with someone who in a certain way positions herself against men, because she feels she has to defend herself, thereby identifying as a victim. Even today I wouldn't call myself a feminist, because I find the term loaded [überfrachtet]." At the same time, Ade notes that because of her experience of running a production company, she's now "thinking more along the lines" of gender issues.[62] She is well aware of how differently male and female film professionals are treated when it comes, say, to assessing the commercial potential of a chosen topic, which is crucial for funding, and she has emphasized that as producer she particularly enjoys working with women. In hindsight, the 2009 Berlinale award ceremony was a possible turning point. While Ade was standing onstage holding her Silver Bear, jury president Tilda Swinton summoned her for a photo op with the Peruvian director Claudia Llosa, the winner of the Golden Bear for *Milk of Sorrow*, and actors Birgit Minichmayr and Magaly Solier by commanding, "only the women!" Swinton's savvy move made Ade realize how impactful the moment was.[63]

Ade's ambivalence about the implications of the term *feminism* is representative of a generation that associates feminism with a certain militancy and a nonconformist cinema. More importantly, most Berlin School filmmakers will agree that the political is defined differently in their films than it was in the New German Cinema— namely, as a counter-cinema committed to modes of refusal and restraint and to a new realism—which is true even for a film with more mainstream appeal such as *Toni Erdmann*. Yet in many ways, today's female film professionals do stand on the shoulders of the German feminist cinema of the 1970s, which successfully advocated for women filmmakers' access to funding, distribution, and the means of production. At that time, as Thomas Elsaesser has noted, Germany had "proportionally more women-filmmakers than any other film-producing country. If this was partially owing to funding sources specifically opened up to women film-makers and women's issues, these opportunities were themselves the result of organized struggles and campaigns."[64] That there is near gender parity between today's male and female Berlin School directors is a further indication of that legacy. And particularly companies like Komplizen Film, committed to making independent features, are indebted to the advances of that earlier generation, even if the demise of the *Autorenfilm* in the mid-1980s and the rule of mainstream cinema in the 1990s make those feminists now seem "uncool."

The activism of the late 1960s, of which the West German feminism of the 1970s is an important part, occurred when Winfried was in his twenties, and the prankster in him certainly preserves some of the period's anarchic creativity. Yet his overall lethargy marks him as an "Alt-68er"—a boomer whose protest days are long over. Nevertheless, Winfried is clearly alert to the (sexist) designs that Ines's male colleagues have on her. After Henneberg has coerced Ines into taking his wife shopping, Winfried embarrasses the CEO by "mistaking" Natalja for his daughter. Sizing up Ines's boyfriend Tim, Winfried observes that he's the son of a car dealer and thus clearly too lightweight for a teacher's daughter. And he literally twice bares his (fake) teeth to protect his daughter from what he perceives as transgressive male behavior by Henneberg and Gerald.

While the role of women in society is a topic on which Ines's and Winfried's views may align, his daughter's professional life clearly follows a trajectory he does not approve of. An important piece in the parenthood puzzle is the cheese grater, one of several finely tuned running jokes in the film. The designer gadget that Ines receives as her birthday present is both a symbol for the affluent society in which she now moves and for the family values put on

Winfried bares his teeth with Henneberg . . .

. . . and with Gerald.

display with a well-prepared meal enjoyed around the dinner table. It is perhaps no accident that Ines sleeps through the one meal Winfried cooks—the spaghetti dinner that would have inaugurated the cheese grater—and thus indirectly tells her father that her career

The omnipresent cheese grater: Ines tries to admire her father's present.

plans will not allow for elaborate home cooking, let alone having a family with whom to enjoy such meals. Ines's spaghetti days, just like the eponymous nickname with which her father repeatedly conjures up her childhood, have passed their expiration date. The cold pasta, thrown into her father's face after his pursuits of her have turned into bona fide stalking, are Ines's rebuke of the cheese grater and all that it stands for. It is this rebuke, not the so-called drug charges, that lands her in handcuffs.

The simmering generational conflict between father and daughter erupts around what constitutes the right way to live. After Ines has humiliated a hotel manager into providing complimentary sand-wiches and champagne to make up for a lousy massage, Winfried, taken aback by her abrasive behavior, asks her if she's actually happy in Bucharest. "What do you mean by 'happy'?" she sharply replies, "like going to the movies, or what?"

Winfried has clearly put his finger on a sore spot. In the age of neoliberalism, everyone is driven to engineer their own happiness. There's a whole industry of self-optimization and self-fulfillment,

When questioned about happiness, Ines gets defensive.

The new colonialists: Ines humiliates a hotel manager.

of which the wellness center, where this exchange occurs, is a prime example (and both Ines's complaint about the bad massage and her push for compensation are driven by her need to get the maximum out of this service industry).

In the new economic regime, happiness is something we can, and therefore must, produce in ourselves, and it is not contingent on other people or external circumstances. Winfried's question about his daughter's happiness is therefore not as innocent as it looks, since it implies a failure of Ines's success at self-fashioning. According to Bjung-Chul Han, real fulfillment is not possible in the new economy, because the achievement subject becomes so consumed with concerns over the performance of the self that it ceases to distinguish those around her as individuals. For the new entrepreneurs, "the negativity of an Other who commands has been left behind."[65] As a result, we encounter a radical form of narcissism: the subject is no longer able to recognize the other *as* Other, which often leads to depression or other disorders. Ines's facetious remark to Winfried, "you and your cheese grater will not stop me from jumping out of this window," fired at him shortly before he departs, might be a veiled admission of deeper personal troubles.

Like many Berlin School films, *Toni Erdmann* focuses on non-happy rather than unhappy protagonists. They lack a certain self-insight, and seal themselves off from those who are eager to provide that insight, which is certainly true for Melanie and to some extent also for Gitti, who rejects the patronizing of Chris's frenemy Hans. Winfried is eager to provide advice, but he is hardly in a position to speak with authority, given his own complacency. The simmering conflict between father and daughter comes to a head when, after Ines has wrapped up her shopping duties with Natalja at the mall, he directly corners his daughter by asking, "are you really a human?"—a comment with which he clearly crosses a line, as it soon leads to a head-on confrontation, and Winfried decides to leave. In a tonal shift typical of the entire film, Winfried senses that his own life philosophy is as fraught as his daughter's. This point is driven home when he gets a worker fired during a visit at an oil production site by reaching out to shake hands, inadvertently drawing attention to the worker's smeared hands, which is in breach of security policies. With

Asking for a time-out, Winfried concedes defeat.

this faux pas, only aggravated by his feeble attempts to make light of the devastating outcome, he de facto becomes the "Unmensch," or inhuman, that he had accused his daughter of being. During the drive back to Budapest, he asks his daughter for a truce. Soon thereafter, after one final stop, he will end his charade, realizing that Toni Erdmann's existence has clearly come to a dead end. In the film's final section, in Germany, he admits to Ines that he himself does not know either what happiness really is, either, thereby conceding that he had no right to ask her to justify her happiness or her humanity.

The professionally ambitious daughter, Jörn Glasenapp has aptly observed, has treated Winfried as "a negative or even repugnant foil and appears motivated by a wholly internalized refusal to become like him."[66] Winfried's remark to Renate early in the film, "we did something wrong," shows that he is aware of that refusal. Yet beyond the generational difference between father and daughter there is, of course, also a significant difference between Winfried and Toni. Indeed, when Winfried becomes Toni Erdmann he undergoes a dramatic transformation that involves more than a wig and oversized teeth. Whereas in Aachen he is lethargic and has heart troubles, his Bucharest alter ego seems reinvigorated and daring—it is a rejuvenation that brings him closer to his daughter's generation, as well as to the circle of professionals in which she moves. As Ade noted, "Toni is a more masculine version of Winfried."[67] It is hard to tell whether this transformation only happens out of desperation to save his daughter from herself, or whether Ines's rebuke, "I know people your age who still have plans," provokes him into action (just as her aside about whoopee cushions makes him go out and buy one). Toni Erdmann is dashing, daring, and a very quick learner, whose new insights about the managerial class become immediate fodder for his stinging parody. There exists between father and daughter a kind of "vampiric psychosocial energy transfer," Glasenapp has suggested: "The deeper Winfried's 'bite' into her life grows, the more Ines is at risk of losing the businesslike bite for which she is known."[68]

The image of the vampire suggests a circulation of blood that affects, of course, both the person doing the biting and the one being bitten. Just as Winfried has channeled Ines—perfecting her poker face, which is so paramount for business negotiations, and using his shaggy gray hair and phlegmatic demeanor for a performance that hides a surprising lucidity and a quick wit—she has taken a page out of his book to respond to the challenge he poses for her life. By inviting him to the "car party" and thereby making him privy to her drug habit, she dares him to drop his disguise and reveal the disapproving father; she similarly raises the stakes when she brings him along to the negotiations at the oil production site as "a colleague"—a visit, as noted, that results in Winfried's humiliation and that leads to the disappearance of Toni Erdmann. The naked brunch scene, which occurs the morning after this excursion, reveals a different affinity between Ines and her father. Her talent for improv and for raising the stakes to call a bluff is, as noted, the most powerful testimony to the prankster hiding beneath *her* controlled veneer. The ensuing embrace between father and daughter in the park is thus the unexpected outcome of an experiment in corporate team building that ultimately builds "team family." Yet, as Maren Ade has noted, this was *not* a scene that could conclude the film, because it suggests a superficial notion of closure.[69]

The ensuing coda in Aachen, which brings the film full circle geographically, revisits some of its key themes, but it does not provide a happy ending. *Toni Erdmann*, Ade has insisted, does not offer "a mode of redemption," reinforcing instead the open-ended nature of her first two features.[70] The balance between apparent circularity and open-endedness is powerfully suggested in *Everyone Else*, which is framed by two scenes in which Gitti plays dead. At the beginning of the film, she encourages Chris's young niece to openly articulate her dislike of Gitti. "Tell me that you loathe me. Tell me!" she provokes the girl—to the point that the girl raises a gun/finger and "shoots" Gitti, who dramatically plunges into the pool and floats facedown for an uncomfortably long period. In the film's concluding scene, Gitti again plays dead, this time by lying motionless on a coffee

Gitti plays dead in *Everyone Else*.

table. While in the first instance, Gitti's make-believe could only last for as long as she could hold her breath under water, in this scene she stubbornly ignores Chris's prodding to wake up, refusing for a long time to stop the performance. When she finally and halfheartedly does, it is left to viewers to decide whether or not this rejection of Chris will spell the end of their relationship.

Even more radical is the ending of *The Forest for the Trees*, when Melanie, desperate to leave behind the confines of job and daily life, gets in her car and drives off into the woods. After a while, she takes her hands off the steering wheel while the car proceeds at full speed and we fully expect a violent crash. More mysteriously still, Melanie then vacates the driver's seat and moves into the backseat, abandoning control in a direct rejection of a society that has not allowed her to fit in, despite (and partly because of) her overeager attempts to conform. The last shot shows her settling in next to the backseat car window and relaxing, as if a burden has been lifted: she has become a spectator to her own life. "The imaginary option of letting the car continue on its own accord," observes Roger F. Cook, "signals that she is ready to become the next in the line of Berlin School protagonists who are content to drift aimlessly, avoiding the choices offered by the new Germany."[71] Both tender and troubling, this surreal moment breaks with the naturalism that dominates the film, which is further ironized by the lyrics, "Welcome back to solid ground, my friend," from Granddaddy's "He's Simple, He's Dumb, He's the Pilot," which carries over into the credit sequence.

As in its first transition between Aachen and Bucharest, the return to Germany in *Toni Erdmann* occurs without any signposting. After a hard cut, the film shows Ines at a memorial service. Many viewers will assume that her father has died, given his heart condition and that he was last seen gasping for air after he had been relieved of the heavy Kukeri mask. (It is telling that Winfried cannot terminate his last performance without the help of others.) With his Toni Erdmann days over, the vitality that this alter ego infused in him

Melanie becomes a spectator to her own life in *The Forest for the Trees*.

Annegret's memorial service is a reminder that death looms everywhere.

may have just evaporated completely. Yet we soon realize that the deceased is actually Winfried's mother Annegret, bringing back to the forefront the theme of mortality that dominated the opening part. Annegret's death introduces a new angle in the generational conflict between father and daughter.

We're dead sad that you're leaving, Mr. Dudinger.

Winfried's students have been coached in his dark humor.

We will recall that the experience of death was forcefully introduced in the opening part of the film, where it is clearly associated with Winfried. His heart rate monitor goes off in the very first scene and then again at Ines's birthday party, indicating a cause for concern. For a retirement celebration at school, Winfried and his students wear makeup inspired by skulls, and his students greet the retiring colleague with the chorus, "We are dead sad [todtraurig] that you're leaving, Mr. Dudinger."

Soon thereafter, Winfried drops off his ailing dog Willi at his mother's, brusquely rejecting her suggestion to have Willi put to sleep by griping, "I don't put you to sleep either." Sounding the same theme, he then wisecracks about making easy money for "mercy killings" at a retirement community—both dubious efforts at comic relief that come across as either dark humor or simply in poor taste. Yet his mother's funeral casts these jokes in a somewhat different light. Because she had first been introduced as a somewhat callous, curmudgeon-like character, Annegret's death clearly impacts Winfried less than Willi's. Winfried's strained relation with his mother takes on a more sinister tone when we learn that, while a fan of Harry Belafonte's music, she still considers it "Negermusik" (Negro music), a derogatory term used by the National Socialists for jazz and swing music by African American performers. When Ines and Winfried rummage through her belongings, they come across a helmet from the Wehrmacht—a very material reminder that the Third Reich, and all it stood for, apparently still had a home at Annegret's. This proverbial skeleton in the closet is a reminder that Winfried and his generation were at pains to fight their parents' complicity in burying the Nazi past and to not allow them to shed their responsibilities for atonement. Ines now realizes that what comes across as Winfried's "pseudogreen mentality" has its roots in a radical rejection of that past, a rejection from which today's German political landscape, as well as her own professional freedom, has greatly benefitted.

At the very end of the film, Ines does a wonderful, brief imitation of Winfried, donning his fake teeth and a fancy hat that belonged to her deceased grandmother. It is a (fleeting) acknowledgment that she has embraced her father's heritage, even if she is staying on course with her career goals. What is more, though, by wearing

Ines's version of Toni Erdmann is a composite of three generations.

something belonging to her father *and* something belonging to her grandmother, Ines's Toni Erdmann is a composite of the two preceding generations, thereby recognizing the ways in which her father's generation was formed in direct reaction to that of his parents', a dialectic that informs her own generation as well. The last shot of the film shows Ines standing by herself, quiet and contemplative, waiting for her father to return with his camera, which never happens. She's on her own now.

The quiet and somber mood of this concluding shot is amped up in the credit sequence, which is accompanied by "Plainsong," a dark and tormenting song by The Cure that evokes solitude and mortality—a startling choice for a tragicomedy, and more proof that Ade considered her film "a melancholy thing."[72] A key lyric, repeated twice, laments: "It's so cold, it's like the cold if you were dead/and you smiled for a second." A postpunk, New-Wave band from Great Britain, The Cure counts as a precursor of gothic rock, with a trademark musical style that is haunting and gloomy. The face of the band is frontman Robert Smith, always performing with disheveled black hair, like Toni's wig, and stage makeup with eyeliner and a pale complexion that resonates with Winfried's grim reaper getup. A contrast to the more conciliatory note on which the film has ended, the credit sequence, with its allusions to death, is yet another instance of the film's radical shift in tone.

"Merkel Kino?"

Toni Erdmann, we have seen, is one of the most critically acclaimed German films of recent years, both in Germany and, especially, abroad—a rare accomplishment indeed. That it achieved this in the guise of a comedy was unprecedented. This extraordinary recognition made it suspect, especially in Germany, where Berlin School films have a track record of coming under fire by critics and fellow filmmakers—in stark contrast to their international reception.[73]

Bernd C. Sucher's polemic 2017 book on Ade's film, *Was ist ein Hype?*, operates on the premise that this much success cannot be legitimate.[74] While Sucher ultimately tries to ride the coattails of that success rather than provide a serious critique, a blog entry by Ade's colleague Christoph Hochhäusler hit closer to home. Under the heading, "Nahtloser Konsens?" (seamless consensus), Hochhäusler accused *Toni Erdmann* of smoothing out contradictions and creating consensus through simplification and stereotypes, classifying the film as a step backward ("Rückschritt") in the director's development.[75] Posing the rhetorical question about whether this kind of cinema is "Merkel Kino," that is, a middle-of-the-road cinema, Hochhäusler declared, "absolutely" (durchaus). The term "Merkel Kino" echoes, of course, Eric Rentschler's influential coinage of a "cinema of consensus," referenced earlier. Coming to prominence during the late Kohl era, that cinema was a tremendously popular genre cinema driven by mainstream comedies and romantic relationship dramas. If we bear in mind that Kohl and Merkel not only belong to the same party but that she started her political career as Kohl's protegée (her nickname was "Kohl's girl"), the thrust of Hochhäusler's polemic becomes especially clear.

The considerable domestic commercial success of *Toni Erdmann*, which echoes the records set at the German the box office by the 1990s comedies, suggests a parallel where none exists. In contrast to Ade's film, most of the earlier hits hardly made any inroads abroad, as their sense of humor did not travel well. Attempts to export titles such as *Der bewegte Mann* (*Maybe . . . Maybe Not*) (Sönke Wortmann, 1994), a standout success of the 1990s, were disappointing failures. What is more, the point bears repetition that *Toni Erdmann* is anything but a straightforward comedy. As Jörn Glasenapp notes, viewers like Hochhäusler, who regard the film as pure a comedy, "fail to see the inherent tragicomedy."[76] Such simplistic classification is indeed more prevalent among German critics. In the Anglo-American world, in contrast, leading voices—ranging from Manohla Dargis, Justin

Chang, and Mark Kermode, to Dennis Lim, Andrew O'Hehir, and Molly Haskell—recognized the film's shifting tonalities and multiple generic registers as well as its emotional and psychological complexity and subtlety.[77]

Hochhäusler's polemic about steps taken backward also raises the larger question about what direction the Berlin School is heading in, both as a movement and in terms of individual directors. In 2013, Hochhäusler had declared that school was out: "Every label carries an expiration date, and to my mind this one has passed. The films of the last few years have veered further and further apart . . ., a development that I find both necessary and liberating."[78] While it remains to be seen in which direction the writer and director Maren Ade is moving, she and her production company are certainly breaking new ground. On the heels of *Toni Erdmann*'s commercial success it was announced that Komplizen Film had sold its rights to Paramount Pictures. In February 2017, *Variety* reported that Paramount had signed Jack Nicholson and Kristen Wig to star in the remake, but both Nicholson and producer Lena Durham withdrew from the project the following year. As of this writing, it is unclear whether or not the project is still under development. While Komplizen Film had reserved the rights to function as executive producers, they are not planning to be more concretely involved in the production.[79]

This hands-off approach appears prudent given the fact that German-language films have generally not fared well when remade in Hollywood. Among a long list of titles a few prominent examples illustrate the point. Wim Wenders's 1987 classic *Der Himmel über Berlin* (*Wings of Desire*) lost all its magic in Brad Silberling's *City of Angels* (1997), despite the star power of Meg Ryan and Nicolas Cage. In 2007, Michael Haneke remade his own *Funny Games* in Hollywood, ten years after its original release. Apart from a few minor changes, the 2007 version is "a doggedly faithful shot-by-shot remake of the Austrian original," Leland Monk observes, and he concludes that the bland American remake only brings into relief what made the original so salient and impressive in the first place.[80] German superstar Til Schweiger, too, was allowed to direct a Hollywood remake of one of his earlier films—namely, the 2014 runaway hit *Honig im Kopf*, released as *Head Full of Honey* by Warner Bros. in 2018. Nick Nolte and Matt Dillon could not save the production from becoming a resounding flop, cementing the point that mainstream German comedy does not cross the Atlantic (or the Rhine, for that matter).[81] A rare exception is the rom-com *Bella Martha* (*Mostly Martha*) by Sandra Nettelbeck (2001). Remade in 2007 by Scott Hicks as *No Reservations* and starring Catherine Zeta-Jones, the film had considerable box office success, earning $43 million domestically and $92 million worldwide.

While selling the rights to a Hollywood remake is unprecedented for a Berlin School director/producer, equally extraordinary is the development of a full-fledged series for a streaming service. The 2019 Netflix series *Skylines*, produced by Komplizen Film and directed by Matt Erlenwein and Soleen Yusef, is one of few German-language series for the streaming giant.[82] Set in Frankfurt am Main, *Skylines* explores over six episodes the world of the German hip-hop recording industry, mixing gang-feud crime drama with police undercover operation and family melodrama, deriving much of its emotional charge from the pumping beats and rhymes of its hip-hop artists. Executive discussions about the radical changes facing the music industry, including the streaming format, the listening habits of young audiences, and getting customers "hooked" on certain artists, lends *Skylines* a charged self-reflexivity about the overall future of the entertainment industry, and especially the film industry. One could well imagine such discussions happening between key members of Komplizen Film, when the unexpected success of *Toni Erdmann* presented them with both new opportunities and challenges. As Komplizen Film producer Jonas Dornbach has stated, "our hearts are still very much with cinema, but new players and platforms appearing on the scene offer new and exciting narrative possibilities."[83]

The city of Frankfurt is more than a background in *Skylines*. Reproduced by kind permission of Netflix Germany, 2020.

While very different from Maren Ade's three films, *Skylines* features a number of details familiar from Berlin School films, among them an emphasis on the itinerant and unmoored nature of modern life. The casting of Richie Müller as a corrupt banker is certainly a nod toward the films of Christian Petzold (the actor appeared in *Cuba Libre*, 1996; *Die Beischlafdiebin* [*The Sex Thief*], 1998; and *Die innere Sicherheit* [*The State I'm In*], 2000), even if for most German viewers Müller will be mostly familiar from his role as police detective Thorsten Lannert in the cult crime series *Tatort*. While generally not boasting a lot of quotations and intertextual references, *Skylines* includes a few direct nods to Komplizen Film's impressive resume: in one scene a key character recovering from a drug overdose watches *The Forest for the Trees* on her laptop, and in another a poster of *Western* adorns a sidewalk. Such insider jokes are subtle reminders that the company behind the series is the same that brought us *Toni Erdmann*.

CREDITS

Director:
Maren Ade

Writer:
Maren Ade

Production Companies:
Komplizen Film
Coop99 Filmproduktion

Produced by:
Maren Ade
Jonas Dornbach
Janine Jackowski
Michel Merkt

Cast:
Sandra Hüller (Ines Conradi)
Peter Simonischek (Winfried Conradi)
Michael Wittenborn (Henneberg)
Thomas Loibl (Gerald)
Trystan Pütter (Tim)
Ingrid Bisu (Anca)
Hadewych Minis (Tatjana)
Lucy Russell (Steph)
Victoria Cocias (Flavia)
Alexandru Papadopol (Dascalu)
Victoria Malektorovych (Natalja)
Ingrid Burkhard (Annegret)
Nicolas Wackerbarth (Coach)
Hans Löw (Oliver)
Julischka Eichel (Babette)
Lennart Moho (Lukas)
Manuela Ciucur (Frau Rodica)

Music:
Gabriel Grote

Cinematography:
Patrick Orth

Film Editing:
Heike Parplies

Production Design:
Silke Fischer

Costume Design:
Gitti Fuchs

Script Consultant:
Valeska Grisebach
Eva Löbau

Runtime:
162 minutes

Sound Mix:
Dolby Digital/Dolby Atmos

Aspect Ratio:
1.85:1

Camera:
Arri Alexa Plus

Negative Format:
SxS Pro

Process:
Digital Intermediate (2K) (master format)/
ProRes 4:2:2 (2K) (source format)

Printed Format:
DCP

Production Costs:
€3,000,000

Release Dates:
Premiere: May 14, 2016 (Cannes Film
Festival); July 14, 2016 (Germany);
August 17, 2016 (France); September 2,
2016 (USA)

NOTES

1   As Ade told Megan Ratner in conversation, in the consultant job "there's this strong aspect of performance involved. You are paid to judge situations and you have to pretend that you know everything." Quoted in Megan Ratner, "*Toni Erdmann*, Faux Pas: Interview with Maren Ade," *Film Quarterly* 70, no. 3 (2017): 46.

2   Tobias Kniebe, "Eine kollektive Erfahrung, die man als Journalist sonst nicht hat: Interview mit Bernd C. Sucher," in *Was ist ein Hype?* ed. Sucher (Berlin: Bertz und Fischer, 2017), 41.

3   Leslie Felperin, "*Toni Erdmann*: Cannes Review," *Hollywood Reporter*, May 13, 2016, https://www.hollywoodreporter.com/review/maren-ades-toni-erdmann-cannes-893953; Guy Lodge, "Film Review: *Toni Erdmann*," *Variety*, May 13, 2016, https://variety.com/2016/film/reviews/toni-erdmann-review-1201773917/.

4   Manohla Dargis, "The Director of *Toni Erdmann* Savors Her Moment at Cannes," *New York Times*, May 22, 2016, https://www.nytimes.com/2016/05/23/movies/the-director-of-toni-erdmann-savors-her-moment-at-cannes.html?smid=nytcore-ipad-share&smprod=nytcore-ipad. With a 3.7 average, *Toni Erdmann* had the highest score to date to be recorded by the influential journal *Screen Daily*.

5   *Film Comment*, 56, no. 1 (January/February 2020): 39.

6   Kent Jones quoted in Danny King, "This Grueling Character Study from Germany Builds to a Radical Conclusion," *AVclub*, March 10, 2015, https://film.avclub.com/this-grueling-character-study-from-germany-builds-to-a-1798277375.

7   Marco Abel, *The Counter-Cinema of the Berlin* School (Rochester, NY: Camden House, 2013), 260.

8   Ratner, "*Toni Erdmann*, Faux Pas: Interview with Maren Ade," 46.

9   Maren Ade quoted in Jan Krüger, "Interview mit Maren Ade," Alexander Verlag Berlin, accessed October 22, 2018, https://www.alexander-verlag.com/programm/texte/1-interview-mit-maren-ade.html.

10 Sean Burns, "*Toni Erdmann*: A Comedy for Those Cerebral Types Who Don't Like Comedies," WBUR Boston, February 26, 2017, https://www.wbur.org/artery/2017/02/16/toni-erdmann.

11 Richard Brody, "A Stilted Vision of a Declining Europe in *Toni Erdmann*," *New Yorker*, December 21, 2016, https://www.newyorker.com/culture/richard-brody/a-stilted-vision-of-a-declining-europe-in-toni-erdmann. For Brody, this lack of visual virtuosity is ultimately a shortcoming of the film because it empties the film of psychological complexity, as he puts it. Brody's position thusrepresents a rare exception to the overall enthusiastic reception of the film in the United States.

12 Manohla Dargis, "Perfectly Happy Until They Venture into the Outside World," *New York Times*, April 9, 2010, https://www.nytimes.com/2010/04/09/movies/09everyone.

html?mtrref=www.google.com&gwh=6A20C4CA489BB5DCE803E856DA432557&g
wt=pay&assetType=REGIWALL.

13 See Coop 99, accessed August 20, 2020, http://www.coop99.at/web-coop99/?page_
id=2303&lang=en.

14 Komplizen Film, accessed October 10, 2019, http://www.Komplizen Film.de/e/
komplizen.html.

15 Mark Peranson, "A Battle of Humor: Maren Ade on *Toni Erdmann*," *Cinema Scope*,
accessed October 22, 2018, http://cinema-scope.com/spotlight/battle-humour-maren-
ade-toni-erdmann/.

16 Ade also credits her own father as model, who, she reports, is in the habit of pulling out
his false teeth to deflate a serious situation or broach a touchy subject. Ade is on record
stating that her parents, like Winfried and Renate, are divorced and have an amicable
relationship, and that both of them are teachers, like Winfried and Melanie from *The
Forest for the Trees*. However, these biographical references contribute little to our understanding of Ade's films.

17 Peranson, "A Battle of Humor: Maren Ade on *Toni Erdmann*." As Ade told Jan Krüger,
"I had a model for 'Ines Conradi's' profession, a [business]woman whom I met and
interviewed in Bucharest. I recorded and transcribed the interviews and had Sandra
[Hüller] read them. Later, she also met this woman" ("Interview mit Maren Ade").

18 Richard F. Shepard, "Songs and a New Comedian Make Lively Cabaret," *New York
Times*, July 11, 1974, https://www.nytimes.com/1974/07/11/archives/songs-and-a-new-
comedian-make-lively-cabaret.html.

19 Various women's reactions to Kaufman's wrestling matches were preserved in a com-
pilation of letters written to the polarizing performer: *Dear Andy Kaufman, I Hate
Your Guts!*, ed. Lynn Margulies (Port Townsend, WA: Process Media, 2009). For an
insightful review of the book, see Farley Elliott, review of *Dear Andy Kaufman, I Hate
Your Guts!*, LAist, November 28, 2009, https://laist.com/2009/11/28/review_dear_andy_
kaufman_i_hate_you.php.

20 DVD extras, *Toni Erdmann*, Eurovideo Medien, Two-Disc Edition, 2016 (Artikelnum-
mer 302823).

21 The official video of the R.E.M. song includes brief clips of Kaufman as Elvis, which are
part of his Caspiar routine, and wrestling with a woman in a boxing ring. See R.E.M.,
"Man on the Moon," uploaded September 13, 2017, YouTube video, 4:51, https://www.
youtube.com/watch?v=dLxpNiF0YKs.

22 See "Andy Kaufman on Letterman," October 15, 1980, YouTube video, 8:42, https://
www.youtube.com/watch?v=6p0sr2BejUk.

23 "Humor entsteht oft aus Verzweiflung oder einer Sackgasse." Ade quoted in Jan Schulz-
Ojala, "'Ich bin eher der misstrauische Typ': Interview mit Maren Ade," *Der Tagesspiegel*,
July 13, 2016, https://www.tagesspiegel.de/gesellschaft/interview-mit-maren-ade-ich-
bin-eher-der-misstrauische-typ/13850252.html. In the same interview, she goes on to
explain the following: "if we can control our sense of humor, it can be a way out, because

it makes it easier to say something or resolve a tension. But after laughter often comes a strangely serious moment, when the mood sinks. The film makes use of this drop ["Fallhöhe"]."

24   Ade has commented on these challenges by saying that, "Peter Simonischek is a very good actor [who] plays Winfried, who's a bad actor who tries to act, and that's a very thin line." See Robbie Collin, "Interview Maren Ade," BAFTA Screenwriters Lecture Series, October 9, 2016, http://guru.bafta.org/maren-ade-screenwriters-lecture-series. The interview can also be viewed here: "*Toni Erdmann* Director Maren Ade: Screenwriters Lecture," uploaded February 9, 2017, YouTube video, 1:09:46, https://www.youtube.com/watch?v=VMV2HuZR3Mk.

25   Andrew Lapin, "*Toni Erdmann:* A Practical Joker Dad and His Too-Practical Daughter," NPR December 28, 2016, https://www.npr.org/2016/12/28/507227395/toni-erdmann-a-practical-joking-dad-and-his-too-practical-daughter?sc=ipad&f=1008?sc=ipad&f=1008.

26   DVD extras, *Toni Erdmann*, Eurovideo Medien.

27   Heinz Drügh, "*Toni Erdmann*: Versuch über Gegenwartsästhetik," *Pop Kultur & Kritik* 10 (2017): 146, accessed Octover 22, 2018, http://www.uni-muenster.de/Ejournals/index.php/pop/article/view/2209.

28   Muriel Cormican, "Willful Women in the Cinema of Maren Ade," *Camera Obscura* 33, no. 3 (2018): 107.

29   Drügh, "*Toni Erdmann*: Versuch über Gegenwartsästhetik," 147.

30   Eric Rentschler, "From New German Cinema to the Post-Wall Cinema of Consensus," in *Cinema and Nation*, ed. Mette Hjort and Scott MacKenzie (New York: Routledge, 2000), 272–73.

31   Rentschler, "From New German Cinema to the Post-Wall Cinema of Consensus," 263.

32   Not surprisingly, Dories Dörrie has joined the chorus of film professionals who have publicly attacked the Berlin School. As she has stated, "I secretly hold against them [the directors associated with the Berlin School] that they do not risk enough and hide behind form. I don't like this: to hide oneself behind form." Quoted in Marco Abel, "Intensifying Life: The Cinema of the 'Berlin School'," *Cineaste* 33, no. 4 (Fall 2008), accessed May 13, 2010, https://www.cineaste.com/fall2008/intensifying-life-the-cinema-of-the-berlin-school.

33   Peranson, "A Battle of Humor: Maren Ade on *Toni Erdmann*."

34   Lubitsch's early broad comedies are full of Jewish humor and quite different from the sophisticated romances he made in Hollywood and that led to his coining the phrase "the Lubitsch touch." A successful Ufa screenwriter known for light fare and musical comedies, Wilder did not direct any films until after he had left Berlin, when he made Lubitsch the role model for his own distinct approach to directing.

35   Nicodemus quoted in Rachel Donadio, "How *Toni Erdmann* Became an Unexpected Comedy," *New York Times*, December 28, 2016, https://www.nytimes.com/2016/12/28/

movies/how-toni-erdmann-became-an-unexpected-comedy.html?smid=nytcore-ipad-share&smprod=nytcore-ipad.

36 A more detailed analysis of Wilder's film, which the director did not consider a comedy at all, can be found in my *A Foreign Affair: Billy Wilder's American Films* (New York: Berghahn, 2008).

37 Ratner, "*Toni Erdmann*, Faux Pas: Interview with Maren Ade," 48.

38 Lapin, "*Toni Erdmann:* A Practical Joker Dad and His Too-Practical Daughter."

39 Hester Baer, *German Cinema in the Age of Neoliberalism* (Amsterdam: University of Amsterdam Press, 2021), 292.

40 A discussion of the neoliberal condition is central to much of the research on the Berlin School. See Abel's *The Counter-Cinema of the Berlin School*, as well as his more recent essay, "'Das ist vorbei': Unzeitgemäße Begegnungen mit dem Neoliberalismus in Christian Petzolds Studentenfilmen," in *Über Christian Petzold*, ed. Ilka Brombach and Tina Kaiser (Berlin, Vorwerck, 2018), 76–99; Jaimey Fisher, *Christian Petzold* (Urbana, IL: University of Illinois Press, 2013); Hester Baer, "Affectless Economies: The Berlin School and Neoliberalism," *Discourse* 35, no. 1 (2013): 72–100; Baer, *German Cinema in the Age of Neoliberalism: A New Film History, 1980–2010*; and Olivia Landry, *Movement and Performance in Berlin School Cinema* (Bloomington: Indiana University Press, 2019).

41 Dennis Lim, "Moving On: The Next New Wave," in *The Berlin School: Films from the Berliner Schule*, ed. Rajendra Roy and Anke Leweke (New York: MoMA, 2013), 90.

42 Petzold quoted in Fisher, *Christian Petzold*, 111.

43 Incidentally, Philipp's secret for success is his plan to game the oil industry, much like Ines oversees the downsizing of a Romanian oil conglomerate to render it profitable for her German client. If one considers the fact that oil is *not* among Germany's considerable natural resources, the neocolonial goals of these German investors become particularly palpable.

44 Grisebach's and Ade's most recent features are part of a larger trend in Berlin School directors to look beyond Germany's borders. Until roughly 2010, the preferred settings had been the German capital and the provinces, yet during the last decade many key directors have ventured further afield. These include Thomas Arslan with his films *Gold* (2013, set in British Columbia) and *Helle Nächte* (*Bright Nights*) (2017, set in Norway); Petzold's *Transit* (2018, set in France); Ulrich Köhler's *Schlafkrankheit* (*Sleeping Sickness*) (2011, set in Cameroon); and *Orly* (2010, set in the Paris airport) and *Der traumhafte Weg* (*The Dreamed Path*) (2016, set in Greece and Berlin), both by Angela Schanelec.

45 Notwithstanding their frequent collaboration, the two directors' approaches to filmmaking differ considerably, with Grisebach working almost exclusively with nonprofessional actors. In contrast to Ade's scripts, Grisebach's are very loosely constructed and she does not give her actors fully formulated dialogue so as to produce a more natural delivery.

46 Gerd Gemünden, "'It's Good to Lose Control': An Interview with Valeska Grisebach," *Senses of Cinema*, accessed March 30, 2019, http://sensesofcinema.com/2019/interviews/

its-good-to-lose-control-an-interview-with-valeska-grisebach/. On the neocolonial dimension of Grisebach's film, see also Codruța Morari, "European Auteurs Revisit the Western: Thomas Bidegain's *Les Cowboys* and Valeska Grisebach's *Western*," *New German Critique* 138 (November 2019): 11–34.

47 Jonathan Crary, *24/7: Late Capitalism and the Ends of Sleep* (New York: Verso, 2013), 10.

48 Byung-Chul Han, *Burnout Society*, trans. Erik Butler (Stanford, CA: Stanford University Press, 2015). It should be noted that burnout is for Han only one of several neuronal illnesses—others include depression and ADHD—that are caused by an excess positivity.

49 Drügh, "*Toni Erdmann*: Versuch über Gegenwartsästhetik," 143.

50 The third richest businessman in Romania (according to Forbes 2019), Ion Țiriac is well known in Germany not only because of his stellar tennis career in the 1960s and 1970s but also because he was the longtime manager of tennis legend Boris Becker. His role in the film can also be seen as an in-joke, because Țiriac's most notable rival on the tennis court was his countryman Ilie Năstase, who plays a prominent role in *Montag kommen die Fenster* (*Windows on Monday*) (2006) by Ade's partner Ulrich Köhler. That film also features Trystan Pütter, who plays Ines's lover Tim in *Toni Erdmann*.

51 David Harvey, *A Brief History of Neoliberalism* (Oxford: Oxford University Press, 2005); Stuart Hall, "The Neoliberal Revolution," *Cultural Studies* 25, no. 6 (November 2011): 705–28.

52 "Regisseurin Ade für Frauenquote bei Filmförderung," uploaded May 14, 2016, YouTube video, 1:29, https://www.youtube.com/watch?v=JU5_zxmL6D0.

53 Michael Richardson, "Bad Sex," in *Berlin School Glossary: An ABC of the New Wave in German Cinema*, ed. Roger F. Cook, Lutz Koepnick, Kristin Kopp, and Brad Prager (Chicago: University of Chicago Press), 43, 44.

54 Drügh, "*Toni Erdmann*: Versuch über Gegenwartsästhetik," 151. While Ade was aware that the scene felt long and potentially boring, she realized during the editing process that she could not cut it, because, if she had, the subsequent one, featuring "Whitney Schnuck," would not have worked. See Collin, "Interview Maren Ade."

55 Lukas Foerster, "Maren Ade: *Toni Erdmann*," *Film Bulletin*, July 22, 2016, https://www.filmbulletin.ch/full/filmkritik/2016-7-22_toni-erdmann/.

56 In an interview, Maren Ade described how Sandra Hüller was to deliver the song: "What I really wanted, was for Ines to sing that song as though she doesn't want to sing it . . . there has to be an option where the way of singing is to say 'fuck you.'" See Steve McFarlane, "Interview: Maren Ade and Sandra Hüller on Making *Toni Erdmann*," *Slant Magazine*, December 19, 2016, https://www.slantmagazine.com/features/article/interview-maren-ade-and-sandra-hueller-on-making-toni-erdmann.

57 Speaking for many reviewers, Claudia Liebrand labeled the song a "pop hymn of self-love." See Liebrand, "Zwei Todesfälle und ein 'birthday suit': Maren Ades *Toni Erdmann*," Literaturkritk.de, November 2016, https://literaturkritik.de/zwei-todesfaelle-und-ein-birthday-suit-maren-ades-toni-erdmann,22647.html.

58 Ivan Kreilkamp, "I Learned to Depend on Me: On Whitney Houston and *Toni Erdmann*," Senses of Cinema June 1, 2017, http://sensesofcinema.com/2017/feature-articles/ whitney-houston-toni-erdmann/. It is furthermore worth noting that Ines knows the complete lyrics of all three stanzas by heart, which lets us assume that this performance is something father and daughter may have done before, when Ines was much younger. Again, Winfried here refuses to treat his daughter as the adult she has become.

59 According to Maren Ade, this idea was not in the script. See Collin, "Interview Maren Ade."

60 Baer, *German Cinema in the Age of Neoliberalism*, 291–92.

61 It should be noted, though, that in Whale's film this innocent encounter turns tragic when the monster drowns the girl.

62 Maren Ade, "Feministin sein war uncool," in *Wie haben Sie das gemacht? Aufzeichnungen zu Frauen und Filmen*, ed. Claudia Lenssen and Bettina Schoeller-Bouju (Marburg: Schüren, 2014), 423. In a 2016 Cannes interview, Ade went on record as favoring a quota system that would ensure gender equality. See Scott Roxborough, "Cannes: *Toni Erdmann* Director Maren Ade Wants a Subsidy Quota for Women Filmmakers (Q&A)," *Hollywood Reporter*, May 12, 2016, https://www.hollywoodreporter.com/news/ maren-ade-directing-toni-erdmann-893318. For a survey on the efforts of contemporary women filmmakers for parity, equity, and more visibility, see Sebastian Heiduschke, "Women's Interventions in the Contemporary German Film Industry," *Camera Obscura* 33, no. 3 (2018): 147–55.

63 See Annabel Wahaba, "'Wir sollen immer nett sein': Ein Gespräch zwischen den Regisseurinnen Maren Ade und Doris Dörrie," *Zeitmagazin*, February 10, 2011, https://www. zeit.de/2011/07/Berlinale-Doerrie-Ade.

64 Thomas Elsaesser, *New German Cinema: A History* (New Brunswick, NJ: Rutgers University Press, 1989), 185.

65 "Es entledigt sich der Negativitität des *gebietenden Anderen*." Byung-Chul Han, *Typologie der Gewalt* (Berlin: Matthes und Seitz, 2011), 38. Emphasis in the original.

66 Jörn Glasenapp, "Mixed Feelings: The Tragicomedy of Maren Ade's *Toni Erdmann*," *New German Critique* 138, no. 3 (2019): 39.

67 Collin, "Interview Maren Ade."

68 Glasenapp, "Mixed Feelings," 44.

69 As Ade noted, "it would have been disappointing to end film there." ("Interview Maren Ade"). Greg Gerke, writing in the *Los Angeles Review of Books*, even calls the actual ending of the film an "anti-Hollywood ending." See "'Toni Erdmann' and the Anti-Hollywood Ending,'" *Los Angeles Review of Books*, March 17, 2017, https://lareviewofbooks. org/article/toni-erdmann-and-the-anti-hollywood-ending/.

70 "Es gibt keine richtige Erlösung." Ade quoted in Schulz-Ojala, "'Ich bin eher der misstrauische Typ': Interview mit Maren Ade."

71 Roger F. Cook, "Disengagement," in *Berlin School Glossary*, 90. See also Brad Prager's entry, "Endings," in the same volume (109–16).

72 Ade quoted in Sucher, *Was ist ein Hype?*, 31.

73 Günter Rohrbach, "Das Schmollen der Autisten: Hat die deutsche Filmkritik ausgedient?," *Der Spiegel* 4 (2007): 156–57; Oskar Roehler, quoted in Rüdiger Suchsland, "Langsames Leben, schöne Tage: Annährungen an die Berliner Schule," *Film–Dienst*, accessed October 8, 2011, https://web.archive.org/web/20051123145625/http://film-dienst.kim-info.de/artikel.php?nr=151062&dest=frei&pos=artikel; Dietrich Brüggemann, "Fahr zur Hölle, Berliner Schule," D-Trick.de, February 11, 2013, http://d-trick.de/blog/fahr-zur-holle-berliner-schule. See also Marco Abel, "22 January 2007: Film Establishment Attacks 'Berlin School' as Wrong Kind of National Cinema," in *A New History of German Cinema*, ed. Jennifer Kapczynski and Michael Richardson (Rochester, NY: Camden House, 2012), 602–8.

74 See Sucher, *Was ist ein Hype?* As Jörn Glasenapp asserts, Sucher's insinuation that the praise was underserved is "both wrong and irritating" ("Mixed Feelings," 36). Of the many contributors to Sucher's collection, the editor is ultimately the only one to claim that the film's success is mostly the product of hype. Among notable German critics, Rüdiger Suchsland has claimed that *Toni Erdmann* does not quite live up to its hype: "Kino-Sensation 2016: *Toni Erdmann* ist ein guter Film—mehr aber nicht," *Rolling Stone* (Germany), December 30, 2016, https://www.rollingstone.de/toni-erdmann-kino-ein-guter-film-mehr-nicht-1172629/.

75 Christoph Hochhäusler, "Nahtloser Konsens?," *Parallelfilm Blogspot*, July 17, 2016, http://parallelfilm.blogspot.com/2016/07/nahtloser-konsens.html. Hochhäusler's remark that the film is not "biting" (beißend) is particularly revealing about how he misreads the complexity of the film's most loaded metaphor.

76 Glasenapp, "Mixed Feelings," 43.

77 Justin Chang, "Comedy and Heartache Make Perfect Bedfellows in the Magnificent German Comedy *Toni Erdmann*," *Los Angeles Times*, December 22, 2016, https://www.latimes.com/entertainment/movies/la-et-mn-toni-erdmann-review 20161216-story.html; Dargis, "The Director of *Toni Erdmann* Savors Her Moment at Cannes"; Molly Haskell, "Toni Erdmann," *Film Comment*, January–February 2017, 46; Frank Kermode, "*Toni Erdmann*: Talk about Embarrassing Parents . . .," *Guardian,* February 5, 2017, https://www.theguardian.com/film/2017/feb/05/toni-erdmann-observer-film-review; Dennis Lim, "Toni! Tony! Toné!" Artforum, June 3, 2016, https://www.artforum.com/film/dennis-lim-on-the-69th-cannes-film-festival-60409; Andrew O'Hehir, "What's the One Great Movie in This Year's Oscar Race?," *Salon,* February 25, 2017, https://www.salon.com/2017/02/25/whats-the-one-great-movie-in-this-years-oscar-race-it-has-a-hairy-bulgarian-monster-and-you-havent-seen-it/.

78 Christoph Hochhäusler, "On Whose Shoulders: The Question of Aesthetic Indebtedness," in *The Berlin School: Films from the Berliner Schule*, 28.

79 Scott Roxborough, "Komplizen Film Trio on Elevating Female Directors and Hollywood's *Toni Erdmann* Remake," *Hollywood Reporter*, May 21, 2017, https://www.hollywoodreporter.com/news/komplizen-film-trio-elevating-female-directors-hollywoods-toni-erdmann-remake-1006013.

80 Leland Monk, "Hollywood Endgames," in *A Companion to Michael Haneke*, ed. Roy Grundmann (Malden, MA: Wiley-Blackwell, 2010), 421.

81 The multimillion-dollar production, which received more than $5 million in German federal funding, made about $12,000, and Schweiger's first Hollywood venture became a humiliating defeat for the ambitious director and star.

82 Tom Tykwer's runaway success *Babylon Berlin* (2017–), with its fourth season now in production, is the rare exception of a German arthouse director finding international success in the streaming series format.

83 Jonas Dornbach quoted in Martin Blaney, "Why the Success of *Toni Erdmann* Prompted a Period of Soul-Searching for Its German Producers," *Screen Daily*, August 8, 2019, https://www.screendaily.com/features/why-the-success-of-toni-erdmann-prompted-a-period-of-soul-searching-for-its-german-producers/5141782.article.